THE DAKOTA APARTMENTS

Vintage Articles of the World's Best-Known Apartment Building

Presented by

Copyright © 2013
Written & Designed by The Cardinals

All rights reserved No part of this publication may be reproduced, stored in a retrieval system, or transmitted in any form or by any means, electronic, media, email, photocopying, recording, scanning, or otherwise, without the prior written permission of the publisher.

While the Publisher and the authors have used their best efforts in preparing this book, they make no representations or warranties with respect to the accuracy or completeness of the contents of this book and specifically disclaim any implied warranties of merchantability or fitness for a particular purpose. Neither the Publisher nor the author(s) shall be liable for any loss of profit or any other commercial damages, including but not limited to special, incidental, consequential, or other damages.

The Campfire Network publishes its books in a variety of electronic formats. Some content that appears in print may not be available in electronic books and vice versa..

Every effort has been made to trace the copyright holders of the photographs and images in this book, but one or two may have been unreachable. We would be grateful if the photographers concerned would contact us so that they make be acknowledged here.

Generosity is something that is always worth appreciating and acknowledging. Due to space limitations we unfortunately can not list the names of every individual who assisted us during the research and publishing process, but we appreciate everyone's kindness and help. With what space we are afforded we would like to express our sincerest thanks first and foremost to the great Andrew Alpern whose wit, wisdom, and knowledge is beyond measure. We would also like to extend our thanks to Lynn Baruch, Stephen Birmingham, Dawn Black, James J. Blum, Delphine Brownlee, John C., Thomas Cathey, Joe Franklin, Rachel Galvin, Christopher Gray, Barry Lewis, Neil McEachern, Richie Ornstein, Jack Perry, Paul Segal, Steve Silberberg, Dara Sperling, Elizabeth Tryon, and Tony Victoria. Sometimes just doing something as seemingly meaningless as answering a quick question made all the difference in choosing the path worth pursuing.

Cover photo: "The Dakota" circa 1895. View from Central Park, east of 8th Avenue.

Published by the Campfire Network
CampfireNetwork.com

Dedicated to:
Jekyll, Autumn, and Bridget
who were, and still are, loved
beyond what any words could fully express.

PART I

The City of the Future. 1879

The Mammoth Family Hotel. October 9th, 1880

Vast Apartment Houses. June 3, 1882

The Dakota. October 21, 1882

Edward Clark's Bequests. October 22, 1882

Plasterer Strike. September 24, 1883

Prominent Buildings Under Way. April 5th, 1884

A Description of one of the Most Perfect Apartment Houses in the World. September 10. 1884

The Dakota. September 20, 1884

The Dakota. February 7, 1885

The Dakota Apartment House. March 7, 1885

The Dakota Stables. 1885

The Wonderful West Side. March 23, 1889

The Sub Surface Courtyard. January 20, 1891

The Dakota Apartment House. 1896/1897

N.Y.'s First Big Apartment House. May 13, 1919

PART II

Edward Clark Biographical Sketch

Isaac Merritt Singer Obituary

Henry Janeway Hardenbergh

PART III

Vintage Photos & Illustrations

For most people around the world, the Dakota Apartments in New York City is mostly known for being the setting of a few interesting Hollywood films, the home of some famous and well-regarded residents, and, unfortunately, the location of some horrible tragedies that occurred there over the course of its unique history.

Through books such as this one we would like to lead people away from any negative memories and perceptions they may have, and encourage them to see the Dakota in the positive, respectful, and dignified manner that it has earned and truly deserves. Simply put, there is much more to know and appreciate about the Dakota, including it major architectural, social and historical significance.

Over the course of the time we spent during our extensive research on the history of the Dakota Apartments we came across many rare newspaper articles that have eluded even the most determined of Architectural Historians and Dakota Scholars. Many that we uncovered will be of great interest to anyone interested in the information provided on one of New York's most legendary buildings.

This volume shares many of the original newspaper articles that were written about the Dakota before, during, and after its design and construction. Many of the articles are beautifully written, with wonderful descriptions, and sing the praises of the Dakota as well as, if not better than, anything contemporary writers have put to words, so we are eager and delighted to share them with you.

We hope you enjoy learning more about the Dakota.

Blue skies!

THE CITY OF THE FUTURE

THE REAL ESTATE RECORD
NOVEMBER 8, 1879

The subject of buildings then coming up, Mr. Edward Clark, one of the largest and most enterprising owners on the West Side, read the following paper which was listened to with great attention:

If the original founders of the city of New York could have grasped the idea that in the course of years, and within a period not great when compared with the usual duration of great cities, the whole island would be surrounded by wharves and warehouses to accommodate the world's commerce, and its entire available area densely covered with buildings to meet the varied wants of a vast population, it is quite certain that the plans for public and private improvement would have been very different from those which have actually prevailed. To suit the convenience of the future city, the most important business of a public nature ought to be concentrated somewhere near the geographical centre of the island.

Draw a line from the North to the East River, through Forty-second street and the intersection of that with the line of Broadway, would indicate not precisely, but somewhat nearly, the place where the Courts, the Exchange, the Custom House, the General Post Office, the large fraternal institutions, and all other business intimately connected with these, ought to be permanently located.

The present existing arrangements are about as inconvenient as could have been devised. There is a daily congestion of the currents of humanity for several hours on the southerly point of the island which is painful to experience or contemplate, and a corresponding depletion toward the evening.

The elevated railways, to a certain degree alleviate this evil, but never can cure it. The struggle of opposing interests is always going on, and cannot be expected to cease until the city is finally completed. Persons who are not yet old can remember when the little triangle called Hanover Square, south of the present Custom House was considered the cluster seat of the greatest trade in the city, and many can recall the time when it would have been thought absurd to try to establish a wholesale business anywhere west of Broadway.

Things look differently now, and there is no reason to suppose great changes will cease to be made. Wall street still gallantly holds its own, but who can tell when or how soon the money changers and their satellites will be compelled to seek other temples.

In our city of the future it seems to me, no single lot on the surface of the island can properly or profitably be spared for a small or inferior building. It is the duty, and ought to be considered a great privilege of the property owners, of the present time, to exercise a judicious foresight as to the manner in which their lots shall be improved and to see to it that buildings erected hereafter shall be permanent in their character.

Looking out from my office window across Union Square I see two very prominent edifices for business purposes – they are the third series of buildings erected on the same sites within a few years – and the most conspicuous and costly private residence in the city stands on the spot where a large and handsome brown stone house was demolished to give it room. The tearing down process has been already carried on to an enormous extent, and there are yet very large districts already built over, where the buildings must be razed to the ground to give place to better. Probably this mushroom-style of building was inevitable during the former period of ignorance and uncertainty. But hereafter there will be no excuse for such improvident and wasteful building.

Considering what has been done, it is not difficult to forecast the future, and the building which is done now can be and ought be such as will be appropriate to the city a hundred years hence. It is fortunate for those interested in this Association that building west of Central Park and above Fifty-ninth street has been so significantly retarded. There is but little except the shanties that requires to be torn down.

I believe some diverse opinions have been expressed in regard to the character of the buildings which ought to be erected on the space between the westerly side of the Central Park and the Hudson River. Some have thought the most profitable course would be to erect small and cheap houses for persons of moderate means. These gentlemen entertain a sincere belief that the wealth and magnificence of New York has exhausted, or will exhaust itself upon Fifth and Madison avenues. But I presume most of the members of this association have a firm belief that the attractive combination of the Central, Riverside and Morningside parks, and the admirable conformation of the land between them, will give this district a sure and distinguished pre-eminence.

Our newspaper paragraphists are very fond of speaking of the merchant princes of New York, and perhaps our wealthy citizens are not averse to being thus designated. No doubt it is true that there are many persons in New York whose incomes are princely in amount, but princes ought to live in palaces, and where are they? To use the idea and language of Gen. Viele, "few persons have thought of constructing anything more than three-quarters of a house."

Gentlemen who have visited Genoa and Venice will remember the palaces which princes who were merchants in former times built in those cities: and from that may form some idea of what merchants who wish to be like princes may hereafter do in the way of construction in New York, particularly if they select the West Side plateau as the scene of their munificence.

The practical question presents itself – how ought the West Side to be improved? We will agree, I think, that it should be built so as to accommodate a great number of families, some splendidly, many elegantly, and all comfortably. That the architecture should be ornate, solid and permanent, and that the principle of economic combination should be employed to the greatest possible extent.

Thus far in the better parts of the city the general plan has been to build single houses, each owner of a lot exercising his own taste, or displaying the want of it, without reference to the wishes of his neighbors, and without any particular regard to the effect of his work upon the appearance of the city.

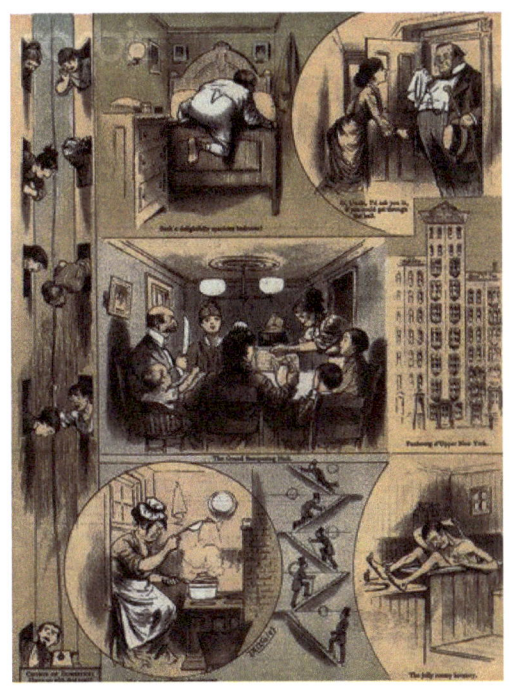

The general plan of apartment houses, or French flats, has been considerably employed in New York, and from the first has met with distinguished favor. Most of them, thus far, have been cheaply built to accommodate people of very limited means. SIt is to be hoped that a new era in building is about to commence, in which intelligent. combined effort will produce novel and splendid results. I will say that for myself, I am in favor of apartment houses for the improvement of the West Side plateau.

Some few have been very thoroughly and elegantly constructed, with a view to being occupied by small families who can afford to expend from five to ten thousand dollars a year. The advantages and economies of these superior dwellings have been so evident that they have always been eagerly taken by excellent tenants as soon as ready for occupancy. The economy will be understood when I state, as probably others can, that I have paid at a leading hotel in New York, for seven or eight consecutive months, at the rate of seven thousand dollars a year for the rent of two small rooms, and that I am able now to rent to others suites of nine rooms, finished in the best possible way, and adopted to all the requirements of elegant housekeeping, for fifteen hundred dollars a year.

There are but few persons who are princely enough to wish to occupy an entire palace, and possibly most of those who are best able to do it, would be most unwilling to take upon themselves the inevitable worry and trouble; but I believe there are many who would like to occupy a portion of a great building, which would be more perfect in its arrangements than any palace in Europe, unless it would be one of very recent construction.

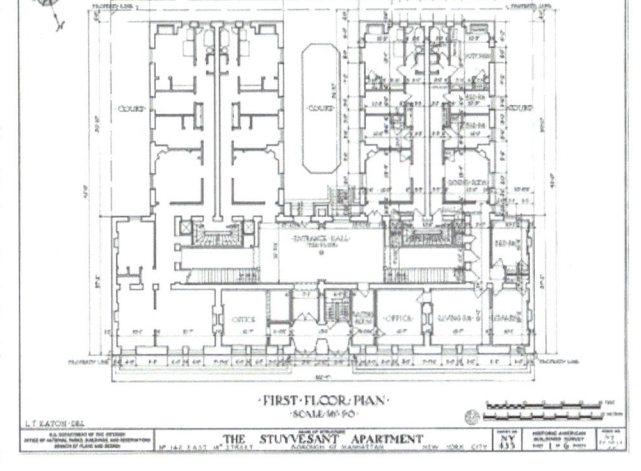

For the principal streets and avenues of the West Side plateau, I should be disposed to advocate the construction of apartment houses, with suites of rooms varying in size and number so as to be suited to the uses of families having the ability to expend from five thousand to fifty thousand dollars or over a year. There is hardly any limit to the rate of expenditure and style of social splendor, to which the apartment house might not easily be adapted, but whatever the scale might be, it is quite certain that for a given amount of money a vastly greater amount of convenience, comfort and display might be secured. There is a considerable class, and such as would be especially desirable on the West Side, who have houses out of the city in which they wish to reside the greater part of the year. To all these the advantages of an apartment in town, into which they could come, and out of which they could go, at any time, are very obvious. But the comparative advantages of apartment houses over single dwellings, though many, I have no time to discuss now.

The corner of 8th Avenue and Broadway, circa 1860s.

The question arises – how are these buildings to be erected, and who are to pay for them? In other cities such houses are built, and certainly the ability exists to construct them here. The first and main point is to establish the necessity for them. The very best and most economical way to prosecute a grand scheme of improvement would perhaps be something like this:

Suppose a whole block on the West Side to have no buildings on it, and the lots to be owned by twenty difference persons, in different proportions. Suppose the time to have arrived when most of these owners are of the opinion that the block should be built upon. Evidently, it is for the interest of all to have their property improved in the best way, and so as to secure the greatest profit. By combining together, employing a single architect and building upon the entire block as one enterprise, the work could be done with much greater economy than by any individual effort, and a splendid result could be attained. As the owners of some of these lots would be much more wealthy than others, those least able to bear the expense of building ought to be able to borrow from the richer as much money as would be required, and at a low rate of interest, as the security would be perfect. When such a building should be completed, it might be divided by commissioners, expert in the business, in accordance with the ownership of the land, and the cost of building might be equitably apportioned in the same way. Thus all parties would be benefited, the wealthier owners by preventing injury to their property by the erection of inferior buildings and the poorer ones by sharing in the advantages of a great capital at moderate interest. The city would gain in the splendid character of the improvements.

This is only a suggestion of a plan, but I feel confident it might be elaborated and put into successful execution. It may be objected, perhaps, that in this outlined scheme no provision has been made for the laboring population. There is the highest authority for believing that the poor will always be with us, but it does not follow that the poor will necessarily occupy any of the West Side plateau. Indeed, I think we should agree that the very poor would be sufficiently with us if they should fix their habitations in New Jersey or on Long Island. But to accommodate the industrious and meritorious working people, the same plans should be pursued substantially as in providing dwellings for the rich.

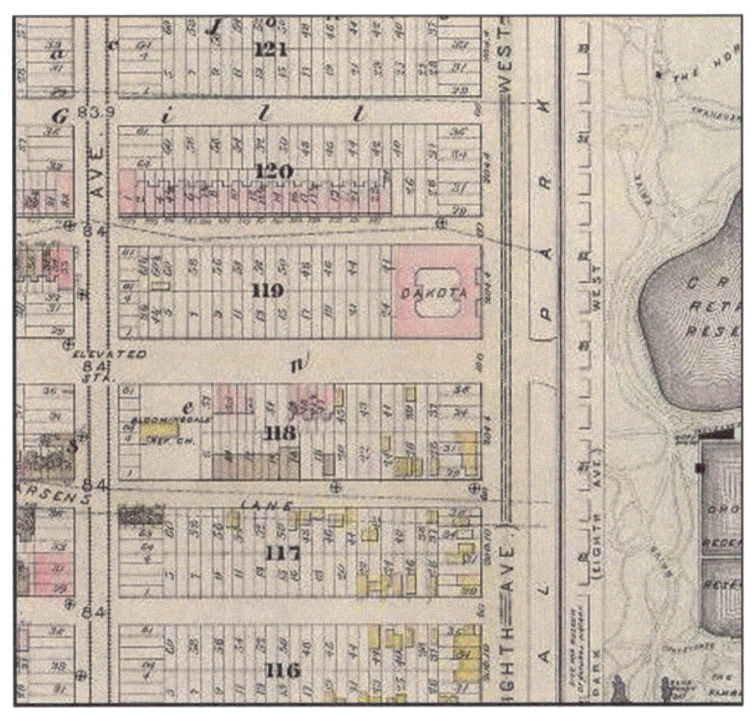

The model dwelling for the poor man should occupy a space, not 25 by 100 feet, but an entire block. It should be quite plain, but solid and substantial in every part. The rooms for each family should be of moderate size and few in number, but every room should have good air and light. Water should be supplied to each apartment or suite of rooms, and they should be heated by steam. The building should be made quite safe as to fire, and a passenger elevator should convey the tenants up and down. All this and more could be furnished to the laboring population, as cheaply as the miserable rooms in tenement houses which they are obliged to occupy now. I suppose the owners of such a model tenement house ought to be, and would be, satisfied with 5 per cent upon the investment, over and above all expenses. In such a case cheapness and very superior accommodations would naturally and easily follow from the vast extent of the enterprise, and the greatly increased number of families who would thus be furnished with homes. The advantages, in a sanitary point of view, of the plans for building, which have been faintly suggested, would be greater than can well be estimated, and it would be easy, as to such dwellings, to exercise a most rigid supervision and effective police.

Probably some judicious legislation might be advisable to aid the formation of combined building associations; but even under the present general laws I believe, with a reasonable and proper feeling among the owners and adjacent lots, whatever is needful might be done to the great mutual advantage of all concerned.

Real Estate Record & Guide
1879

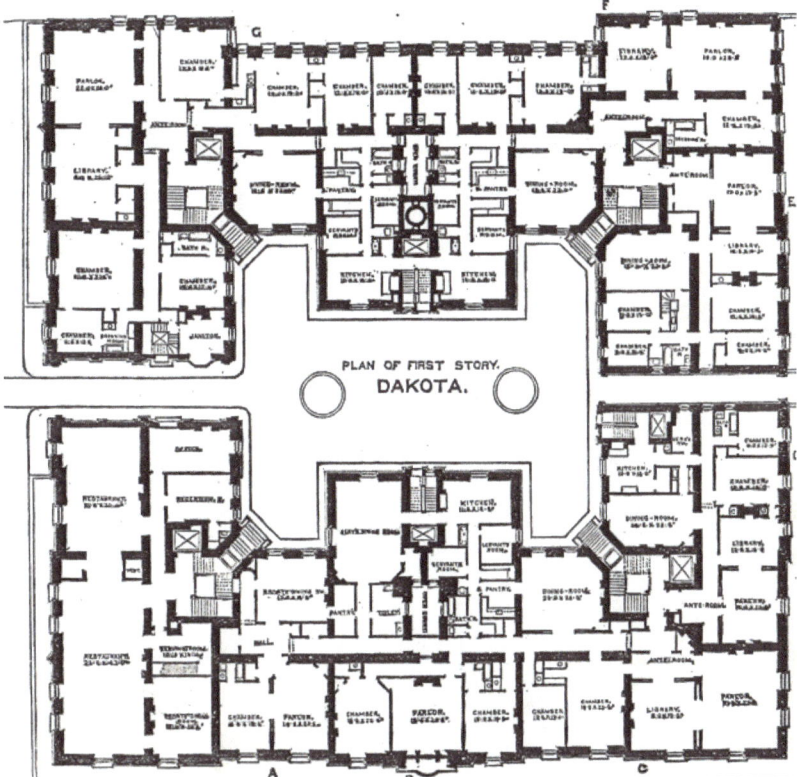

The Mammoth Family Hotel

THE REAL ESTATE RECORD
OCTOBER 9, 1880

Two years, at least, will be required for the completion of the grand family hotel for which the foundations have just been laid on the Eighth avenue, between Seventy-second and Seventy-third streets. The situation is, indeed, unsurpassed, it being high ground facing Central Park, and on the broad street forming the great connecting link with Riverside Park.

Of course, it is well known that Mr. Edward Clark, President of the Singer Manufacturing Company, and a large holder of West Side real estate, is to carry out this enterprise. He has a double object in erecting this extensive building, namely, to give an impetus to the improvement of the West Side, as well as to define the character of the buildings which should grace it, and to offer the city such a hotel as it is now greatly in need of, where persons of means can find a home equal in all its comforts and luxuries to our first class private dwellings, surpassing them in location and without their entailed discomforts and inconveniences; in short, such a place of residence as can be found in some of the capitals of Europe, where persons of the highest rank occupy the different clagex of similar family hotels, and live in great elegance.

In this country the conditions of living are different from those of all other countries except England, requiring the appointments of such an hotel to be superior to those of like buildings abroad, and it is the intention to make this one more complete in every detail of comfort, luxury and elegance than any yet erected.

The building has been designed by Mr. H. J. Hardenbergh, and will be erected under his supervision. It will be nine stories in height above the basement, will occupy the whole frontage of 204 feet of the block on Eighth avenue, and present a front of 200 feet on each of the streets named. The style will be Renaissance, of the period of Francis 1st. The materials of fronts will be Nova Scotia stone and flue pressed brick, the former profusely used, handsomely moulded and carved. In plan the building encloses a large court, the pavement of which is on a level with the street and having an opening on the north side extending from the pavement to the roof line.

The main entrance in on the south (or Seventy-second street front), through a broad, open arched driveway into the court, in the four angles of which are the entrances and stairways to the different suites of apartments. The rooms for the porter or concierge open on this passage and command a view at all times. On the north front is a second or inferior entrance for persons on foot only. On the west side of the building will be a driveway running through from street to street, and this will be inclined to the level of the basement floor and be for the service of the building and of the tradespeople. Under the main court will be a second court reached by the driveway just named, where all the working of the great house may take place unseen.

There will be between forty and fifty suites of apartments, of sizes varying from five to twenty rooms, all of large proportions. On the main floor, fronting Eighth avenue and Seventy-second street will be a fine restaurant comprising main dining hall and private dining rooms. This will have an entrance from the street direct, and will offer accommodations to transient visitors as well as to persons living in the house. Many of the suites will be arranged with kitchens attached, others with dining rooms only, so that it may be optional with tenants whether they are served from the restaurant or not.

The basement will be devoted to kitchens, engine rooms, janitors apartments and private storage rooms; the attics to servants rooms and laundries. The building will be entirely fireproof in every part and constructed in the most thorough manner. Seven large hydraulic elevators will run to different floors and as many staircases of iron and marble will be placed in different parts of the buildings. The woodwork throughout will be of the finest varieties in use, in many cases elaborately finished. The building will cost over a million dollars.

Real Estate Record & Guide
October 9, 1880

VAST APARTMENT HOUSES

THE REAL ESTATE RECORD
JUNE 3, 1882

Unless all the indications are deceptive, before five years are over New York will have the largest and best appointed apartment houses in the world. Every week some new plan is filed, and the last design has some attractive novelty not thought of when these great establishments were first erected. In one of the projected Madison avenue Paris flats there is to be a garden on the top; another proposes to have a Turkish or Russian bath for the use of its inmates. Mr. Jose F. de Navarro's series of houses on Fifty-ninth street will contain many novel features, as will also Mr. Clark's "Dakota" on Eighth avenue and Seventy-second street. The most magnificent scheme of all, however, is that of Mr. W. H. Post. His project is not yet in a shape to present in all its details to the public, but enough is known to settle the fact that it will be the most ambitious structure of the kind in the world. It is to be located near the Central Park, probably on the West Side, and will cover an entire block. There will be two hundred suites of rooms, each occupying on an average 25x85 feet space. It is understood that the Astor estate is interested in this great scheme, which is to be something more than a mere place of residence, for the projectors have in mind certain co-operative features. It is intended to supply certain articles of food for daily use at wholesale prices. Coal will be bought by tie boat load and distributed, dressed meat or cattle will be contracted for at wholesale rates, and every effort will be made to furnish needed supplies at a minimum cost, the object being to abolish the corner grocery man, and save to householders the profits they now pay out to the minor stores.

There is a report in circulation that Mr. James Gordon Bennett intends to erect the finest hotel in the world upon a portion, if not all the block bounded by Fifth and Madison avenues, Thirty-eighth and Thirty- ninth streets. As the buildings on the ground are too valuable to be removed, they are to be utilized in a sort of composite structure, and thus will be afforded a great variety of apartments for the guests of the hotel, the lessees of which will be the gentlemen who now have charge of the Brevoort House. This last hotel, by the way, will probably be abandoned, and the building put to some other use, as it is out of the region travelers care to patronize ; it may indeed be made into an apartment house. It is known that Mr. Bennett has acquired some adjoining property to his house on Fifth avenue. As much as two years ago he contemplated erecting an apartment house. It may be that the large payment to his sister, in settlement of the estate, 'may interfere with his building designs. Rich as he is, the raising of nearly $700,000 in cash must be somewhat of a strain upon him.

The demand for suites of rooms in apartment houses is far in excess of the supply. It is understood that, although far from completion, the Dakota, belonging to Mr. Clark, on Eighth avenue, is bespoken to the extent of two-thirds of its accommodations. Quite a number of Mr. Navarro's apartments are also already engaged. Among the immense structures which have been filed at the Building Department since the first of January are the following. A perusal of this list will give our readers some idea of the vastness of the buildings, and the large sums of money to be laid out in their construct ion. It will be seen that if these buildings multiply, New York will soon contain more palaces than all the capitals of Europe.

Northeast corner Broadway and Sixty-second street, eight-story, 116.2x139.11x100.5 x87.1. Owner. Abraham Benson. Cost, $500,000.

Southwest corner Park avenue and Sixty-second street, nine story brick and brown stone, Byzantine style, 100.5x85. Owner, William Van Antwerp. Cost, $175.000. Architect, W. H. Cauvet.

North side of Seventy-second street, 100 feet east of the Boulevard, eight-story brick and brown stone, Venetian style, 90x90. Owner, William V. A. Mulhallon. Architect. W. H. Cauvet. Cost, $125,000.

Southwest corner Seventh avenue and Fifty-seventh street, seven-story, commenced about fifteen months ago by William F. Croft. Now owned and being erected by William Noble. Cost, $250,000.

Fifth avenue and Twenty-eighth street, southeast corner, 100x125. Owners, Stock Company. Architects, Hubert Pirsson & Co. Cost, including the ground, $1,000,000.

North side Seventy-second street, 250 feet west of Third avenue, seven-story brick and Dorchester stone, 39.6x93. Owner, William Noble. Architect, Geo. W. DaCunha. Cost, $75,000.

Northwest corner Ninth avenue and Seventy-eighth street, eight-story brick and terra cotta, 102x100. Owner, James O'Friel. Architect, E. Gruwe. Cost, $250,000.

Northeast corner Madison avenue and Thirtieth street, ten-story brick, 91.6x110. Owners, G. P. Lowrey et al. Architects, Hubert Pirsson & Co. Cost, $300,000.

Fifty-seventh street, north side, 75 feet east of Sixth avenue, seven-story brown stone, 69.5x90. Owner, Jacob B. Tallman. Architect, H. J. Dudley. Cost, $200,000.

North side Seventy-sixth street, 185 feet east of Madison avenue, 60x92, seven-story brownstone. Owner, Frederick Aldhous. Cost, $90,000.

Northeast corner Fifth avenue and Twenty-eighth street, nine-story brick and brown stone, 75x150. Owner. Stock Company. Architects, Hubert Pirsson & Co. Cost, $850,000.

Nos. 40 and 42 East Twenty-fifth street, six-story brick and terra cotta, 50x86.8. Owners, The Barrington Association. Architect, Carl Pfeiffer. Cost, $100,000.

Northwest corner of Eighth avenue and Forty-sixth street, two five-story brick, one 85x73, the other 40x83, to cost respectively $120,000 and $60,000. Owner, John Jacob Astor. Architect, Thomas Stent.

Southwest corner of Broad way and Fifty- fourth street, seven-story, 52x71.5x75.5. Owner, Victor B Dispurris. Architect, A. B. Ogden.

Nos. 12 and 14 West Eighteenth street, six-story brick and brown stone, 58 x half the block. Owner, a stock company. Architect, August Hatfield: cost, $120,000.

Northwest corner of Eighth avenue and Sixty-second street, nine-story brick and stone, 100x115. Owner, a co-operative association. Architect, Carl Pfeiffer; cost, $250,000.

By far the most extensive improvement in the shape of apartment houses is the proposed erection, by Mr. Jose F. De Navarro, of ten mammoth houses on the plot of ground between Fifty-eighth and Fifty-ninth streets, and east of Seventh avenue. These houses will all be nine stories high and the material to be used is granite, brown stone, Ohio stone and Milwaukee and Philadelphia brick. They will be in the Moorish style of architecture, and it is estimated that the total cost of construction will be $3,000,000. Contracts have just been signed for the construction of the four houses nearest to Seventh avenue and which are to be known as the Lisbon, Madrid, Cordova and Barcelona. These houses are to be divided by passageways 25 feet wide, above which there will be easy means of access, on every floor, from one house to the other in case of any sudden conflagration. The halls and stairways will all be lined with enamelled brick, which does away with the use of laths, plastering, etc. Mr. R. Deeves has been appointed general superintendent and work was commenced on these four houses on June 1st, and it is confidently stated that they will be completed in sixteen months from that day. Out of the fifty-two apartments, all have been sold but thirteen. About August 1st work will be commenced on four more of these houses, and the erection of the remaining six houses will be pushed as soon as possible. The architects are Messrs. Hubert, Pirsson & Co., and the agents, Messrs. Lespinasse & Friedman.

In this connection we may mention that Mr. Edward Clark's family hotel, the Dakota, will be completed by next spring at a cost of nearly $1,500,000. It is eight stories high, built of brick and Dorchester stone and covers the entire front on Eighth avenue from Seventy-second to Seventy-third street, 204.4x200. Architect, H. J. Hardenburgh.

Real Estate Record
June 3, 1882

THE DAKOTA

THE REAL ESTATE RECORD
OCTOBER 21, 1882

The latest,
the largest
and the costliest,
. . . of the apartment houses
is thus far
the most successful architecturally.

This is the "Dakota,"

in Eighth avenue, extending from Seventy-second to Seventy-third streets, and about the same distance to the rear, so as to make it nearly a square of 200 feet, Mr. Hardenbergh is the architect, and he has had the benefit of the experience of previous designers of apartment houses, including his own, an experience which has certainly not been lost upon him.

The building encloses a large court, visible from the outside through a narrow opening in the north wall, and consists, architecturally, of three fronts, one on each street and one on the avenue. The problem of securing repose without monotony and animation without restlessness, in so large a building was not an easy one, but it has been solved.

Each front is treated in a manner by itself, so that none is the repetition of another, but there is not difference enough to interfere with the unity of the total impression from any point of view. Thus the north side has two gables near the centre, the east front two gables at the ends, the south front one gable in the centre, over the large archway which is the principal entrance.

Each wall is distinctly divided into beginning, middle and end. A basement of two stories, the openings of the first square headed, and of the second round arched, is separated by a broad and decorated band of light stone or terra cotta from the main wall, which consists of four stories treated nearly alike. Then comes a shell frieze of terra cotta and over this a narrow balcony upon which the windows of the seventh story open, while there is an eighth story in the roof itself.

Not the least attraction of the building is its color yellow or rather salmon colored brick from Perth Amboy with olive sandstone from Nova Scotia, a combination almost unique here and very agreeable.

The stone is used in quoins at the angles of the projecting masses crowned by the gables, in the coping of these gables, in the arches and jambs of the openings and in belt courses.

There are besides two well designed oriels in stone, curved in plan, each running through six stories on the south side. The expression of the building, as we have said, is at once sober and animated, and this expression is heightened by the skill and restraint with which the detail is designed. This is, in the main, a reminiscence of French Renaissance, used with freedom and intelligence.

There are, naturally, drawbacks to the complete success of the building. The detail, never offensive or extravagant, is here and there flat and thin, notably in the main entrance, which sadly lacks depth, and it is sometimes irrationally applied, as in an overlaying of "architecture" upon the uppermost story of the east front, which projects beyond the plane of the wall below.

The architect must regret, now that he sees the work in place, that he permitted himself to diversify one story of his oriels with meaningless pilasters; and it is questionable whether he ought not to regret that he did not still further emphasize the division of the beginning of his building from the middle, by making the whole basement of stone.

The projections of the gabled pavilions are too shallow to be fully effective; and indeed, we might sum up the shortcomings of the building by saying that it lacks depth and force of modeling. But these are shortcomings only, be it noted, in the expression of an idea and the execution of an architectural design, upon the success of which, in spite of the shortcomings, the architect of the " Dakota" is to be heartily congratulated.

Record & Guide
October, 1882

EDWARD CLARK'S BEQUESTS

COOPERSTOWN, OCT 21.- EDWARD CLARK BEQUEATHED $50,000 TO WILLIAMS COLLEGE. THE OTHER LEGACIES WERE: TEN THOUSAND DOLLARS EACH TO JAMES BUNYAN, OF COOPERSTOWN, AND JAMES MEEHAN, OF NEW YORK, HIS AGENTS; TO MRS. ALFRED CORNING CLARK HIS DAUGHTER IN LAW, $250,000; TO EACH OF HIS GRANDSONS $250,000; TO EACH OF HIS TWO NEPHEWS, SONS OF NATHAN CLARK, OF ATHENS, N. Y. $60,000. WITH THE EXCEPTION OF TWO FINE FARMS ON OTSEGO LAKE AND SOME REAL ESTATE IN NEW YORK CITY, THE VAST BULK OF HIS IMMENSE ESTATE GOES TO HIS ONLY SON, ALFRED CORNING CLARK, OF THIS VILLAGE. JAMES BUNYAN AND JAMES MEEHAN ARE EXECUTORS.

THE NEW YORK TIMES
OCTOBER 22, 1882

PLASTERERS CALLED OUT.
THE STRIKE AT THE DAKOTA FLATS BECAUSE NON-UNION MEN ARE EMPLOYED.

The delegates from the Executive committee of the Amalgamated Building Trades Unions called at the Dakota flats yesterday morning and had an interview with Mr. Meighan, one of the Executors of the Clark estate, and with Mr. Banta, the builder. They repeated their demand that the non-union plasterers should be discharged unless they joined some union. Messrs. Meighan and Banta replied that the plasterers were employed by Mr. Powers, with whom a contract for plastering had been made, and they had no control over his men. Mr. Powers refused to discharge them, because he was satisfied with their work, and should they undertake to interfere with him he would sue them for damages. The delegates thereupon ordered all the union workmen to take up their tools and seek work elsewhere, Some ugly lead pencil marks were made on the fresh white plastering, which will have to be cut out and laid over again. This malicious mischief, it was said, was done by the strikers. Mr. Krebel, the architect, said that although Mr. Powers had no connection whatever with the other row of buildings in the same, street, belonging to the Clark estate, the union had bailed out all the workmen, there, simply because Mr. Banta happened to be the builder there also.

The greater part of the plastering on the Dakota flats has already been completed. About 30 plasterers were at work in the upper stories yesterday, and with these Mr. Powers says he will be able to finish the job on time. A considerable part of the wood-work has also been done, and about 20 carpenters who would not join the union were working. Mr. Krebel said that the work in the flat was already so far advanced that part of the apartments would soon be ready for tenants, and the remainder could be gradually completed by comparatively few workmen. The; delegates retired in ill-humor, and threatened to call out all the workmen employed in all the buildings of the Clark estate.

The New York Times
August 24, 1883

Prominent Buildings Under Way

REAL ESTATE RECORD
APRIL 5, 1884

The "Dakota" is at last near completion, and is receiving its finishing touches prior to its opening in May, when it will be quite ready for dwelling purposes. This huge structure is ten stories and basement in height, and has a total frontage of over 600 feet, 204.4 feet on the avenue and 200 feet on both Seventy-second and Seventy-third street. It contains fifty six suites of apartments, with two to twenty rooms in each, there being about five hundred rooms in all. It is expected that when the building is fully occupied that some three thousand people will reside in it, including the army of servants and other auxiliaries. The material is of brick and Nova Scotia stone. A novel feature will be that the building will be lighted throughout by electricity, supplied by a machine of 600 horse power. This will communicate also with the row of buildings belonging to the Clark estate on the north side of seventy-third street, which will also contain electric lighting, being probably the first instance on record where the new light will be used for domestic purposes on so large a scale, that means some thirty houses in all. The building has eight Otis elevators, four passenger and four freight. The principal contractors are: John L. Banta, mason; T. Brien, plumber: Post & McCord, ironwork; J. L. Hamilton, carpenters; J. Gillis & Son and Henry Wilson, stonework, and Potter & Stymus and others, woodwork. It may be interesting to note that the highest pinnacle on the " Dakota" is 185 feet. The architect is H. J. Hardenbergh, who states that the building when completed will have cost over $1,000,000.

The DAKOTA:
A Description of one of the Most Perfect Apartment Houses in the World

THE REAL ESTATE RECORD
SEPTEMBER 10, 1884

Probably not one stranger out of fifty who ride over the elevated roads or on either of the rivers does not ask the name of the stately building which stands west of Central Park, between Seventy-second and Seventy-third streets.

If there is such a person the chances are that he is blind or nearsighted. The name of the building is the Dakota Apartment House, and it is the largest, most substantial, and most conveniently arranged apartment house of the sort in this country. It stands on the crest of the West Side Plateau, on the highest portion of land in the city, and overlooks the entire island and the surrounding country.

From the east one has a bird's-eye view of Central Park. The reservoir castle and the picturesque lake, the museums, and the mall are all shown at a glance. From this point also can be seen Long Island Sound in the distance, and the hills of Brooklyn.

From the north one looks down on High Bridge and the tall reservoir tower, which looks as slender as a needle.

From the west can be seen the Palisades, the Orange Mountains, and the broad Hudson, which narrows into a silver thread as the double row of hills close together far away in the distance.

Looking south one sees the tall towers of Brooklyn Bridge, Governor's Island, and far beyond the green hills of Staten Island and the blue waters of the Lower Bay.

Every prominent landmark in the landscape can be distinguished from this location, and the great buildings of the lower city are as prominently marked as if the sightseer were floating over the island in a balloon.

At this elevation every breeze which moves across Manhattan from any direction is felt. This is a feature which needs no emphasis to make attractive such stifling days as these.

The building is of the Renaissance style of architecture, built of buff brick, with carved Nova Scotia freestone trimmings and terra cotta ornamentation. Although there is a profusion of ornament in the shape of bay and octagon windows, niches, balconies, and balustrades, with spandrels and panels in beautiful terra cotta work and heavily carved cornices, the size and massive construction of the edifice prevent any appearance of superfluity.

The building is about 200 feet square and 10 stories high, the upper two stories being in the handsome mansard roof which, with its peaks and gables, surmounted by ornate copper work cresting and finials, and relieved by dormer and oriel windows, gives the entire structure an air of lightness and elegance.

The construction is of the most massive character, and the aim of the owners has been to produce a building monumental in solidity and perfectly fireproof.

The brick and mason work is of unusual weight, the walls being in some places four feet thick, and the partitions and flooring have iron beams and framing, filled in with concrete and fireproof material.

On the Seventy-third-street side there is a handsome doorway, and on the Seventy-second-street front [there is] a fine arched carriage entrance, with groined roof and elegant stone carving. Both entrances lead into the inner court, from which four separate passages afford access to the interior of the building.

From the ground floor four fine bronze staircases, the metal work beautifully wrought and the walls wainscoated in rare marbles and choice hard woods, and four luxuriously fitted elevators, of the latest and safest construction, afford means of reaching the upper floors.

The ladies' sitting room, adjoining the staircase in the southeast corner, will be decorated by the Misses Greatorex, a guarantee that the work upon it will be artistic and unconventional. There are four iron staircases and four elevators inclosed in massive brick walls and extending from the cellar to the kitchens and servants' quarters in the upper stories, separate from the rest of the house, which can be used for domestic purposes, carrying furniture, merchandise, &c. There are electric bells to each elevator, and a complete system of electric communication throughout the house. The building is in four great divisions, which inclose a courtyard as large as half a dozen ordinary buildings. This gives every room in the house light, sunshine, and ventilation.

Under this courtyard is the basement, into which lead broad entrances for the use of tradesmen's teams. Here are situated the most interesting portions of the building, or at least the most novel ones. The floor is of asphaltum, as dry and hard as rock. This basement, also, has a courtyard as large as the one above, and lighted by two huge latticed manholes, which look like a couple of green flower beds in the stone flooring. Off of this yard are the storerooms of the house, in which the management will store the furniture and trunks of the tenants free of charge. A porter is assigned to this duty alone. The rooms are all marble floored, lighted and heated, and accessible at all hours of the day or night. The rooms of the servants are also on this floor. These consist of separate dining and toilet rooms for the male and female servants and a male reading and smoking room. These are not for the personal servants of the tenants, but for the general help of the management, which will not number far from 150 persons.

The laundry, kitchen, pantry, and bake shops, and private storerooms are here also, for the owners combine a hotel with the apartment house, and furnish eating facilities for all the tenants of the building who prefer it on the table d'hôte plan.

Opening from the lower court, and extending under the open ground in the rear of the building, a large vault, 150 feet long, 60 feet wide, and 18 feet deep, is now being excavated. When finished it will contain the steam boilers, steam engines, &c., for hoisting, pumping, &c., and the dynamos for supplying electric illumination in the Dakota and adjoining 27 houses. The vault will be roofed with iron beams and brick filling arches and made flush with the land in the rear of the building, 225 feet deep, which will be laid out as a garden. The boilers, with the furnaces, machinery, &c., will thus be located outside the walls of the building safely remote.

The first floor contains the dining rooms, which are finished in a perfect manner. In this case these words really mean something. The floors are of marble and inlaid. The base of the walls is of English quartered oak, carved by hand. The upper portions are finished in bronze bas-relief work, and the ceilings are also quartered oak, beautifully carved. The effect is that of an old English baronial hall, with the dingy massiveness brightened and freshened without losing any of its richness. The effect is heightened by a large Scotch brownstone engraved fireplace, which ornaments the centre of the room.

The business office has oral communication with every portion of the house, and the wants of the tenants can be attended to as quickly as can be done by human ingenuity and a perfectly arranged service.

In addition to the four staircases mentioned before, which are finished in bronze and marble, there are four iron staircases for servants, four passenger elevators, and four servants' elevators.

The Dakota will be divided into 65 different suites of apartments, each containing from four to twenty separate rooms, so that accommodations can be furnished either for bachelors or for large families.

There is an air of grandeur and elegance not only about the halls and stairways but also about the separate apartments that cannot probably be found in any other house of this kind in the country.

The parlors in some instances are 25 by 40 feet, with other rooms in proportion, and there are in many cases private halls to the suites, furnished with fine bronze mantels, tiled hearths, and ornamental open fireplaces.

The parlors, libraries, reception and dining rooms are all cabinet trimmed, paneled, and wainscoated in mahogany, oak, and other attractive and durable woods, and are furnished with carved buffets and mantels, mirrors, tiled hearths and open grate fireplaces, and parqueted floors.

The kitchens are spacious, and provided with ranges, with ventilation hoods, all with Minton tiled facing and marble wainscoating. There are porcelain washtubs, large storerooms and closets, and butlers' pantries, equipped in the most complete manner, and each suite has its private bathrooms and closets, fitted with the most approved scientific sanitary appliances.

The plumbing and hygienic arrangements are fully equal to anything in this country. On the top story are six tanks, holding 5,000 gallons of water each, and supplied by steam pumps having a daily capacity of 2,000,000 gallons, and about 200 miles of pipe have been used in effecting its circulation. Not only in the sanitary appliances, but in every other department, there is a completeness that is surprising. the precautions taken to secure proper ventilation and a pure atmosphere, to insure safety to occupants in cases of fire or panic, and to extinguish fire are perfect.

When opened the comfort and convenience of the guests will be further insured by the accommodations of the dining rooms, laundry, and barber's shop, run to the most improved plan, in connection with the building. It is the perfection of the apartment style of living, and guarantees to the tenants comforts which would require unlimited wealth to procure in a private residence. The wisest precautions have been taken to insure freedom from the ordinary cares of the household to the fortunate tenants.

For instance, the coal and kindling wood are purchased by the manager in large quantities and sold to the tenants, who take in exchange for their money tickets which are presented at the office, and the fuel is carried to their rooms in convenient quantities, thereby saving the user from any of the necessary troubles in buying and storage. This may seem like a small matter, but it is only one of the hundred plans taken by the owners to secure the comfort of the tenants.

It is almost needless to state that the building is as nearly fireproof as any which can be erected.

There are continuous passageways extending through the four divisions on the roof; ninth, eighth, and first stories.

On the tenth floor there is provision for a play room and gymnasium for the children, well lighted and ventilated and commanding a grand view of the city and surroundings, while on the ninth floor there will be extra servants' rooms, private laundries and drying rooms, dormitories for transient male and female servants and attachés of the building, and lavatories, toilet rooms, and bathrooms for their use.

The work on both the Dakota and the neighboring apartment house and private dwellings owned by the estate has been done not only in the most careful manner, but with a view to permanence and convenience, and to symmetry as well as beauty of appearance. The greatest skill and experience and the best materials large means could command have been employed, and the manner in which the work in each department has been done reflects the greatest credit on those entrusted with it, especially upon the architect, Mr. H.J. Hardenbergh, who has supervised the work from its commencement to its now rapidly approaching completion.

Both the Dakota, the private residences, and the smaller apartment house are now ready for occupation, and we need hardly comment on the peculiar attractions they will possess for those who have experienced a desire for an eligible residence on the west side.

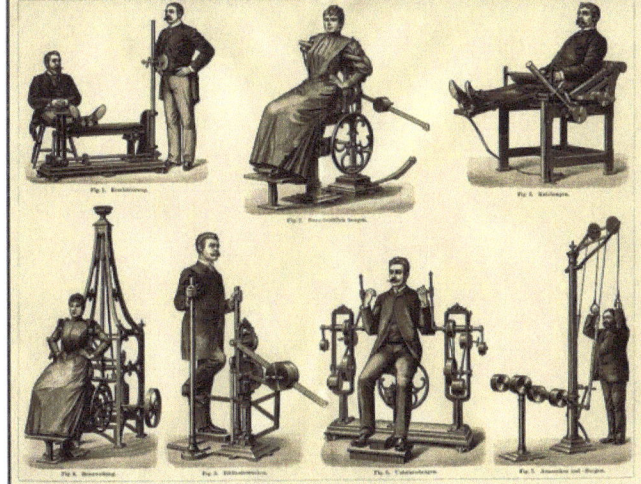

The natural and artificial attributes of the position are all in favor of the buildings, which for comfort, ample space, salubrity, convenience, and accessibility cannot be excelled, and a glance at our description will suffice to show that everything skill could furnish, ingenuity and experience suggest has been supplied.

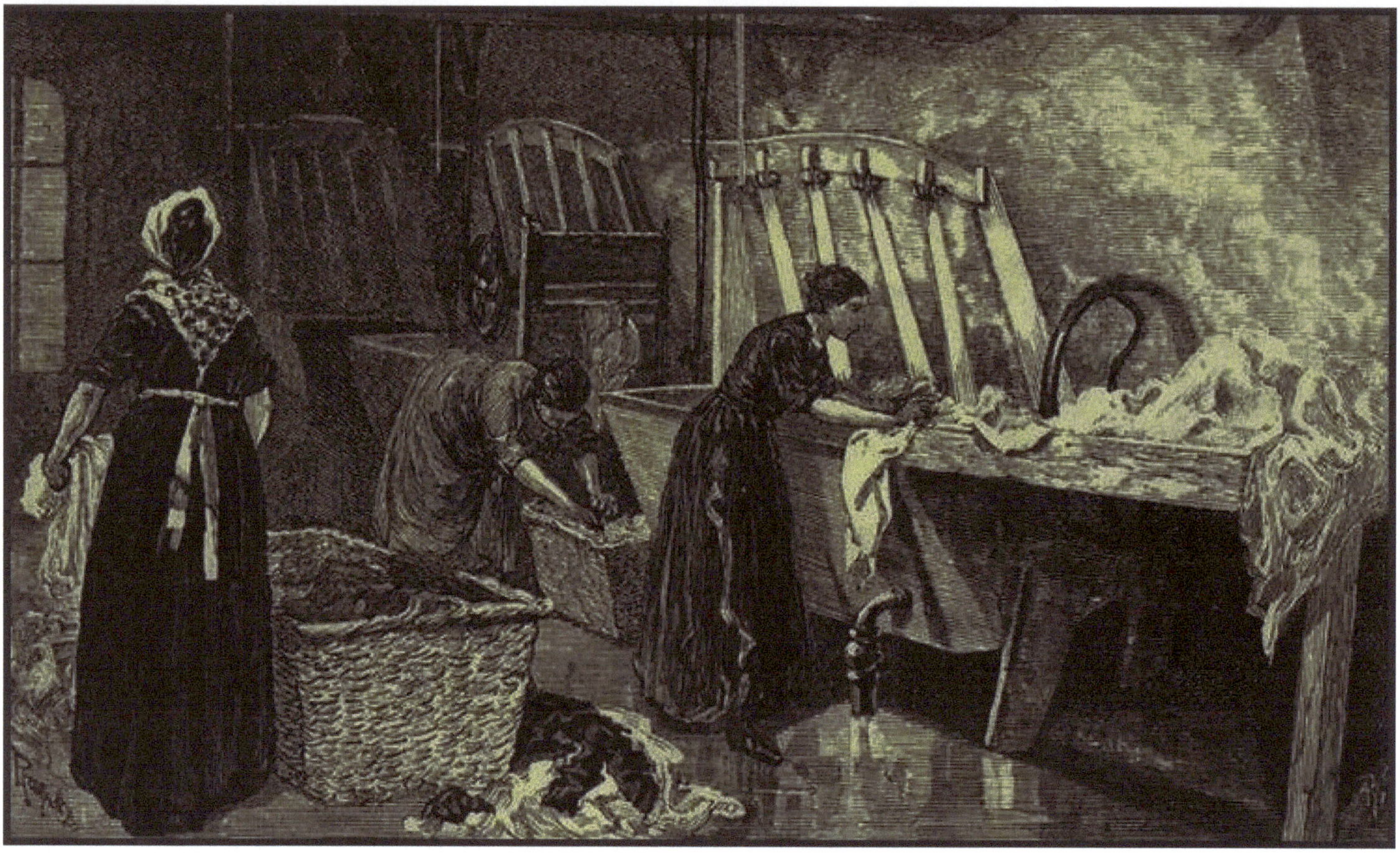

The managers of the Clark estate, the owners of the property, are well known for their fairness and liberality to tenants, and every care will be taken to insure comfort and wellbeing. The rents are moderate when compared with the accommodations furnished, and those desiring to secure either dwellings or apartments can examine plans, &c., and make arrangements at the office of the estate, at No. 25 West Twenty-third-street, New York.

The Daily Telegraph
Sept. 10, 1885

THE BRUSH ELECTRIC LIGHT STATION—STREET ILLUMINATION IN NEW YORK.

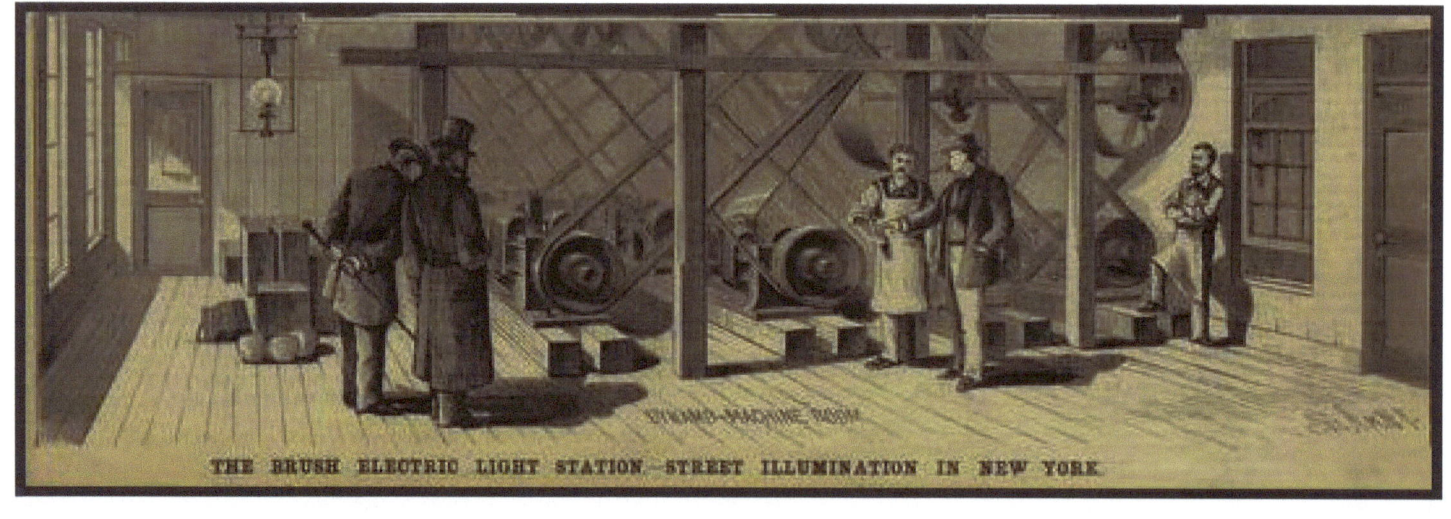

The Dakota

THE REAL ESTATE RECORD
SEPTEMBER 20, 1884

We have heretofore spoken in high praise of the architecture of the Dakota apartment house, a species of design which is here so successful that we are apt to forget the extreme difficulty of the problem.

The Dakota is, indeed, the most successful, architecturally, of all the apartment houses, although the enormous Navarro houses are successful also in securing dignity without monotony.

We mentioned when the Dakota was still far from completion what seemed the principal shortcoming of its design, a defect of vigor in the modeling of the parts. This is still evident, and it seems also that the building would have gained in clearness of division if the two stories of the basement had been built throughout of stone.

Notwithstanding this, the division is clear, and it is to this cleverness of division and to the careful study, which has been given to the relation of its principal masses that the Dakota owes the real nobility of its general impression. This impression is enhanced by an extremely fortunate combination of color in the Nova Scotia stone and salmon-colored brick of which it is composed, and by the appropriate and constructional use of these colors, the stronger tint everywhere going with the structural emphasis; and it is not injured by the treatment of detail, though this latter is seldom exquisite.

Everybody knows the building and we need not waste space in description. It is worth while pointing out, however, how thoroughly it conforms to the Aristotelian precept of being divided into a beginning, a middle and an end, and to the other precept, which Aristotle omitted to lay down, that one of these principal divisions should be superior in magnitude and importance to the rest.

Vertically this requisite is secured in the first place by the grouping of the two lower stories, the upper being distinguished by round arched openings and by a somewhat more copious use of stone than has been employed elsewhere, although, as we have intimated, a still freer use here, or perhaps an exclusive use of the stone, would have been still more effectual to differentiate the basement from what is above it. It is, however, sharply set off from the wall above by a heavily molded string course of stone, and the spandrels of the arches are filled with a frieze in terra cotta of very nearly the same strength of color with the stone.

The principal wall contains four stories of square-headed openings, similarly treated, but rescued from monotony by the differences of arrangement laterally.

Above this is the cornice line, emphasized on the projecting parts of the building by corbelled balconies above an arched frieze of yellow terra cotta of an unfortunately glaring tint, which is no mellower in color now than when it was put up two years ago. Above this is the varying outline of the roof, with a row of dormers in the curtain walls, and with one or two or three tiers of windows in the walls of the terminal gables.

The treatment laterally differs with each front, but it is so skillful that the variety thus secured seems to have come of itself, and has no look of being forced or capricious. The long opening in the centre of the Seventy-third street front is an apparent exception to this remark, since it is hard to see why an opening, of which the only purpose is to admit sunlight and air into the central court of a building, should be cut through the only front from which the sunlight can never reach the court.

Nevertheless, the composition of this front, with the steep gables flanking the opening, is very effective, and even piquant, without any derogation from its dignity.

Of the other two fronts the eastern, facing the park, is much the most conspicuous, or will be when the block south of Seventy-second Street is built up, but it is by no means so well composed as the southern front. The central feature, with its roof hipped back, is too large for its place, and too nearly equal in importance to either of the two gabled masses, which terminate the facade. If it were narrower and the space thus saved given to the curtains between the centre and the ends, the front would gain in repose whereas now it is crowded with the three large masses divided by insufficient intervals.

The Seventy-second street front is a capital composition. The gabled mass at the centre, containing the principal entrance, is clearly the dominant feature of the facade, the masses at the ends not coming in any way into competition with it, but securing a completely harmonious whole.

Above this is the cornice line, emphasized on the projecting parts of the building by corbelled balconies above an arched frieze of yellow terra cotta of an unfortunately glaring tint, which is no mellower in color now than when it was put up two years ago. Above this is the varying outline of the roof, with a row of dormers in the curtain walls, and with one or two or three tiers of windows in the walls of the terminal gables.

The treatment laterally differs with each front, but it is so skillful that the variety thus secured seems to have come of itself, and has no look of being forced or capricious. The long opening in the centre of the Seventy-third street front is an apparent exception to this remark, since it is hard to see why an opening, of which the only purpose is to admit sunlight and air into the central court of a building, should be cut through the only front from which the sunlight can never reach the court.

Nevertheless, the composition of this front, with the steep gables flanking the opening, is very effective, and even piquant, without any derogation from its dignity.

Of the other two fronts the eastern, facing the park, is much the most conspicuous, or will be when the block south of Seventy-second Street is built up, but it is by no means so well composed as the southern front. The central feature, with its roof hipped back, is too large for its place, and too nearly equal in importance to either of the two gabled masses, which terminate the facade. If it were narrower and the space thus saved given to the curtains between the centre and the ends, the front would gain in repose whereas now it is crowded with the three large masses divided by insufficient intervals.

The Seventy-second street front is a capital composition. The gabled mass at the centre, containing the principal entrance, is clearly the dominant feature of the facade, the masses at the ends not coming in any way into competition with it, but securing a completely harmonious whole.

The oriels on either side effectively relieve the expanse of wall. The iron roofs of these oriels are not as successful as some of the detail, but the treatment of them was especially difficult. The projections are everywhere slight, but they are sufficient to account for the interesting and picturesque variety in the treatment of the roofs, and they are made the utmost of by being quoined in stone, with which the gables are also coped, and thus the projecting masses distinctively outlined. Among the minor excellencies of design is the care which has been taken to keep an ample pier not only at the corner of the whole pile, but at the flank of each important feature, by grouping the openings towards the centre, a disposition which greatly enhances the sense of solidity.

The planning of the Dakota is very interesting, but our present business is with the architecture, and the only opportunity for a treatment of the interior, which can properly be described as architectural, was in the design of the restaurant, which occupies the southeastern corner on the ground floor. This consists of two large rooms on the Seventy-second street front, including the corner room, and a smaller square room on the Eighth avenue front. This last is wainscoted and ceiled in mahogany, while the other two are united in treatment, the materials being oak, stained "antique," and bronze. The former material is used in a high wainscot and in the ceiling, the latter in the field of the wall. The high wainscot is paneled with a molded base and a richly carved frieze, admirably designed and perfectly executed. The ceiling, which is coffered, is a particularly happy piece of design, being solid and constructional in effect while stopping distinctly short of the heaviness, which a constructional treatment of a timber ceiling is apt to impart. The wall is of plaster, molded in a diaper pattern and at present uniformly bronzed. The effect of color is sober and rich, but a trifle easily be relieved by a few touches of color if the room is found to require it when finished, The features of the apartment are two heavy and rich chimney pieces in sandstone, and a large sideboard in carved oak, all rational, scholarly and skillful in design.

A feature worth noting is the lining of the fireplaces, which is in cast-iron, a grotesque and successful reminiscence and combination of Italian Renaissance and Japanese treatment.

The faithfulness, indeed, with which the design has everywhere been carried into detail, and everything thought about, is extremely satisfactory, as well as the liberality with which the architect's designs have been executed. The only noticeable piece of frugality is the substitution of red brick in the basement walls on the north side for the far more effective rough-faced stone which is used elsewhere. This, however, is scarcely worth mention, in the evidence which the Dakota everywhere gives in abundance both that the owners have been fortunate in their architect, and that Mr. Hardenbergh has been fortunate in his clients.

Record and Guide
September 20, 1884

The " Dakota" is ten stories high, eight of which are used for living purposes. It contains three frontages of 3oo feet, on Eighth avenue, Seventy-second and Seventy-third streets. It contains fifty-eight suites of apartments, and is estimated to have cost between $1,500,000 and $2,000,000, though the latter figure is probably nearer the mark.

The rents range from $1,000 to $5,600. If entirely occupied, the rentals would yield $150,000 per annum. The running expenses amount to about $40,000, which would be increased to $50,000 or more if all the suites were occupied. At present, however, scarcely half have been rented.

The net return on the cost of the building would be about 4 per cent, if all tenanted. Of course the "Dakota" may be regarded as an exception to the majority of apartment houses, as it was built not for speculation, nor to be disposed of at a large profit, nor with the object of being rented at high figures. The late Edward H. Clark had in view the erection of a noble structure, to be erected as an ornament to the west side, as well as for the accommodation of the affluent, and where architectural beauty was paramount, expense was ignored, with the result that the " Dakota " stands to-day unsurpassed amongst the apartment houses of the city. It may be added that the building is free from mortgage, is fire-proof, and insured at from fifteen to forty cents for three years. The architect was H. J. Hardenbergh.

Real Estate Record & Guide
February 7, 1885

The Dakota Apartment House

THE REAL ESTATE RECORD
MARCH 7, 1885

We present our readers to-day with a picture of this immense apartment house. The Dakota is one of the largest structures of the kind in the world. It may aptly be termed the "mammoth" apartment house, on account of its size and the area it covers. It is an imposing structure. It towers high and above every up town building on the west side, and viewed from an altitude is one of the principal objects for miles around.

It over-looks the Central Park, and has a total frontage of 808 feet, 204 on Eighth avenue, 200 on Seventy-second, 200 on Seventy-third street, and 204 to the westward, where, owing to the private park adjoining, its light will be unimpeded by structures opposite. In the matter of light, situation and dimension, the Dakota is unsurpassed by any apartment house in the city.

Noble in appearance as is the exterior, it is necessary, in order to gain an approximate idea of the size, to explore the interior. Here, the visitor is lost, as it were, in immensity. Room after room is passed, until their numbers appear legion.

The inside is approached through a carriage drive, with groined ceilings, leading to a large open court, 55x90, accessible to each of the eight entrances leading to the different floors of the building.

There are fifty-eight suites, containing eight to twenty rooms each, renting from $1,000 to $5,600 per annum, and there are six hundred and twenty-three rooms in all.

The largest in the building is the dining-room, and for its size, 25x95, the handsomest on Manhattan Island. The ceiling is in finely carved English quartered oak. The fireplaces are quite a feature, being some fifteen feet high, and composed of a pleasant looking Scotch brown stone, doing special service for this purpose, while the tiling is in Mosaic.

Standing at the end of the chamber and gaining a perspective an idea of its size is obtained, and should the guests of the Dakota ever feel disposed to have a ball, they will find ample space for dancing on the polished floors of this spacious apartment. Adjoining is a private dining-room for the accommodation of the guests should any of them desire to entertain their friends in privacy. The room is elegantly fitted up in mahogany, while the wall covering is of a fireproofing material of handsome design in imitation of majolica. A large beveled glass window appears to the west, and when lit up produces a fine effect. We now turn into the ladies' reception room. This is the gem of the house; not in size, be it said, but in richness of adornment. It forms an exception to every other room in the building, in so far as the work is the art of feminine hands. Nine curtains adorn the chamber. Five of these are of satin, covered with elegantly painted flowers and leaves in oil, the remainder being of dark green plush velvet, the furniture covering to match. The frieze is beautifully decorated with clematis, the tendrils leaning over gracefully towards the door. The handiwork of this room is wholly that of the sisters Greatorex, with the exception of the clever etchings on the walls, which were drawn by the mother of those ladies.

We now ascend one of the four grand staircases leading to the upper portion of the building. The wainscoting is of the choicest marbles, each panel being of different color and design. A broad strip of Mexican onyx surmounts the whole, and forms a striking relief to the more somber tints by which it is surrounded. The balusters from top to bottom are of a pretty design in iron, and resting here awhile we peer up into the heights to catch a glimpse of the tenth story.

We now ascend one of the handsome elevators and step out opposite one of the largest suites in the house.

The drawing room is approached through a vestibule some twelve feet square, containing a well designed and finely wrought grate and mantel in iron. This chamber is 24x30 in dimension. The trim is of mahogany, and the floor parqueted. It contains a very handsome chandelier of unique design in brass, with appliances for gas or electricity, exclusive of four additional brackets of similar design in different parts of the room, which contains altogether some forty electric lights. Adjoining, entered through massive sliding doors, is a reception room, 18x20, in mahogany, with elegant mantels; and beyond this is a library, 19x24, fitted up similarly. Then comes a ladies' boudoir, 15x27.

To describe each chamber in the suite would occupy too much space, but suffice it to say that in addition to these rooms there is a large dining-room, 18x24, carved in oak, directly opposite the drawing-room, and beyond the library are no less than nine bedrooms, varying in size from 14x23 to 22x23, bathrooms, toilet, dressing and billiard rooms, servants' apartments, butler's pantry -- in fact, twenty rooms in all. A glance at some of the other suites displays similar elegance and size, though many are of more modest pretensions, containing half the number of rooms of that described.

One of the features of the building is the great length of the halls, from which access is gained to each room. It is quite a little promenade to traverse them from end to end. They are 170 feet in length on each floor and 5 feet in width. We now ring the bell for the elevator and ascend to one or the highest altitudes on Manhattan Island. Once on the roof, a splendid view meets the eye. Being a clear day we can see 36 miles westward, 25 to the northeast, and 20 to the south.

In the distance the Orange Mountains are seen, at our feet are the Hudson River and the Palisades: the bay, with Staten Island in the distance, looms up before us, while high bridge, the Obelisk, and Hell Gate are on the one side, and huge apartment houses and other buildings appear towards the south, flanked by the Brooklyn Bridge.

But the prettiest sight of all—one well worth seeing last week – was the thousands of skaters on the Central Park lakes moving to and fro, looking like Lilliputians from that great height, while the hundreds of sleighs with their tinkling bells, the long string of carriages and other vehicles, combined with the general surroundings, made the seen most picturesque.

Turning from this feast of the sight, we proceed to examine the roof of the building, which is quite a little hamlet in itself. It is all copper-plated, with the exception of the gables, which are tiled in slate. Twelve large tanks are situated on different corners. Portions of the roof, those for instance overlooking the Central Park and the Palisades, would make an excellent retreat in summer time from the heat indoors, owing to the refreshing breeze, which forever blows at such an altitude.

Having explored the heights, a peep into the depths may not be uninteresting. One touch of the electric bell and an elevator comes sailing up at our beckon call and we descend into the lower regions of the Dakota.

We commence by entering the boiler room. Here are eight tubular boilers supplying steam power for the building, and we found workmen engaged continually shoveling coal into the furnaces. The engineer on being asked how much coal had been used during the proceeding twenty four hours replied, "twenty-two tons." The most interesting room is that containing the electrical apparatus. The dynamos have a capacity of 120-horse power. The whole is under the care and supervision of an expert electrician, and as dusk was drawing nigh we were just in time to witness the machinery commence to work preparatory to conducting the light to the building.

The writer was accompanied by a representative of the Clark estate and by Mr. Chatterton, the courteous manager, who very intelligently answered all queries addressed to him. Passing by the large laundry and ironing room, 25x80, we came upon the pump roam, size 22x60, where we saw the machinery in operation having a capacity of 2,000,000 gallons per diem.

Then comes a store room, bakery, pastry-room, dish room, larder-room, and the kitchen, 25x70, from which a ventilator, eight feet in diameter, runs to the top of the building. There are various other rooms for the use of servants, and we must not forget the barber shop, where we peeped in to see some of the guests being submitted to the tender mercies of the tonsorial artist.

Ascending to the office on the first floor, an immense number of electric bells and speaking tubes meet the eye. These give the manager control of all the employees in the building from that spot, and enables him to communicate with every corner of the structure. The writer asked for an example of the efficiency of the system, and it was at once practically demonstrated to him. The bell was pressed communicating with the man running the eastern elevator. The signal was immediately returned. A question was put to him through the speaking tube communicating with him, and his reply came back at once in clear and audible tones. It was but the work of half a minute.

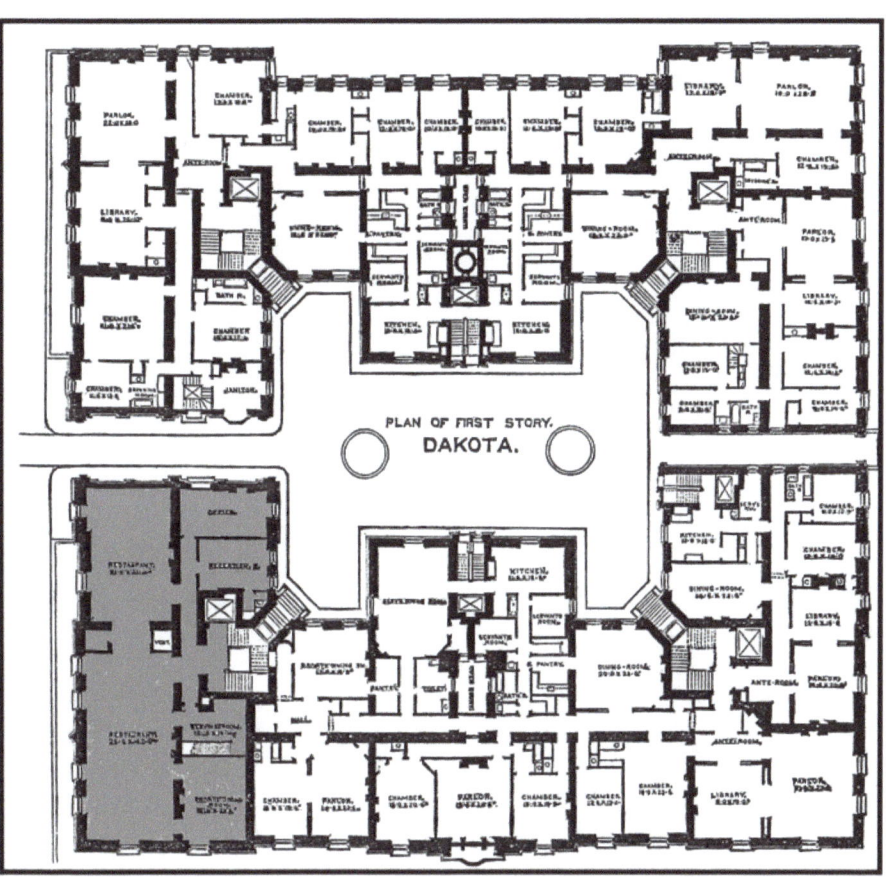

PLAN OF FIRST STORY, DAKOTA.

Speaking of the electric light, which is in every room of the building, it may be added that 4,000 electric lights are distributed throughout the Dakota and 300 electric bells. There are special private wires communicating with all the fire stations, together with a telegraphic instrument enabling an operator to converse with the various fire stations, and also wires to the Dakota stables, telegraph and messenger offices, florist, etc.

The building is in hard-wood trim and contains steam heat throughout. The chandeliers all over the house are of elegant design and have alone cost many tens of thousands of dollars.

The plumbing is of a sanitary character and the ventilation and light is unsurpassed. The building contains four passenger, and four servants and freight elevators.

The Dakota is estimated to have cost between $1,500,00 and 2,000,000. It is thoroughly fireproof—that is, as fireproof as human ingenuity could possibly make it—and this has been recognized by the fire insurance companies, who have rated it at from fifteen to forty cents for three years. Though free from mortgage, the taxes, assessments and running expenses will amount to about $50,000 per annum when fully occupied, though a large number of suites are still to rent. The arrangements in every part of the structure are perfect, and every possible accommodation that can minister to the comfort and happiness of human beings is provided, regardless of labor and cost.

To describe in detail all the features of this immense structure would be impossible in the limited space at our command, but the above sketch will give the reader some idea of one of the noblest apartment houses in the world.

Real Estate Record & Guide
March 7, 1885

THE "DAKOTA" STABLE, NEW YORK CITY, MESSRS CHARLES W. ROMEYN & CO., ARCHITECTS.

This structure forms part of a scheme started some years ago by the late Edward Clark, and since continued by the estate, for the improvement of the "West side", bordering on Central Park. The building is intended to afford stable accommodations for the many tenants of the estate and for the general public of the neighborhood who, until its completion, have been without such a convenience. The walls of the building are started on a base of dressed bluestone, Croton brick and terra-cotta being employed above to the line of cornice, which, together with the dormers, is of copper. A prominent feature in the plan is the entrance court, thirty feet by thirty feet in size, the walls of which are lined with imported enameled brick. From this court ingress is obtained to the carriage floors. By an easy incline horses ascend to the second floor, which contains the stalls. The third floor is divided by a large hall at each end, and contains space for storage of feed and carriages. The construction is of the most substantial kind, and the ventilation is perfect. The total cost (including blasting for cellars, etc.,) was $70,000.

American Architect & Building News
Volume 17, 1885

The Wonderful West Side

ITS CHANGE IS A MARVEL TO THOSE WHO KNEW IT IN ITS DESOLATION

**THE SUN
MARCH 23, 1889**

A Splendid New City Built Up Where Five Years Ago There Were Only Rocks, Swamps, Goats and Shanties • Substantial Tenements, Comfortable Apartments, and Handsome Private Residences for the People • There Wasn't Room for in the Overcrowded East Side • The Elevated Railroad Has Done Much, But Additional Facilities for Rapid Transit Would Work New Wonders • Going To Keep Right On Growling And Improving The Real Estate Men Say.

It is a truism to say that the growth of the west side of this city has been and is simply marvelous. Within the last five years a territory which was only known to New Yorkers as being but little better than a wilderness of rocks and goats and swamps and shanties, which inspired the most desolate feelings in the beholder, has, metaphorically, blossomed like the rose and become the scene of a great addition to the city's life. The rocks have vanished, the swamps have become solid earth, and the goats are all dead. The homes of modern New York are up there now. Thousands of beautiful and substantial structures stand in place of the rickety shanties. The city west of Central Park, between Fifty-ninth and Ninety-sixth streets has really become a new city, as unlike the rest of New York almost as the rest of New York is unlike Boston or Philadelphia. So quickly has this been accomplished that many people cannot yet believe that it is a fact. As they have gone up town on the

Ninth avenue elevated road they have seen the busy little steam drills puffing away with ceaseless vigor at the big masses of rock all around; but there seemed so much of the rock and so little of the steam drill that the latter, after all, was only apt to provoke a smile. It seemed as though to get the rock out of the way would be the work of a life-time. But the rock is nearly all gone- at least between the streets referred to-and there are houses of brick and stone, flats, tenements, apartment houses, and private residences is their place.

The SUN presents to its readers this morning a graphic illustration of the progress made in building on the west side of the city during the last five years. The diagram speaks for itself better than any words or description can speak for it. In comparison with the buildings erected since 1884 those erected before that time seem almost insignificant in number. They seem to hang feebly to a corner or to be built at haphazard in the middle of a block. Even real estate men and others familiar with the great strides made in building in the last few years will probably be surprised at this exhibit of the number of houses built in this time. Before 1884 there were hardly any substantial houses at all between Eighth Avenue and the North River, and between Seventy-fourth and Ninety-sixth streets. There was a little cluster of brownstone fronts in Ninety-third Street, between Eighth and Ninth avenues. These, the most ambitious houses in the neighborhood, were erected by Boss Tweed in the vain attempt to start building in that portion of the city. Today they are about the worse looking building up there. Between Seventy-fourth and Fifty-sixth streets there were few houses on the side streets. There were no houses on Eleventh avenue, but two or three houses on Eighth and Ninth avenues, and but few more on Tenth avenue. While the building now is around Ninth Avenue as a centre, before 1884 Tenth Avenue seemed likely to become the great popular thoroughfare. The two triangular pieces of land between Seventieth and Sixty-sixth streets, and between Seventy-third and Seventy-fifth streets formed by the two intersections of Tenth Avenue and the Boulevard, were quite covered with houses.

Houses were at the street corners for a good distance up the broad avenue. But there was nothing like solid blocks of flats and apartments and tenements and private residences. The building was all desultory and scattered. The great Dakota flats erected years before on Eighth avenue, between Seventy-Second and Seventy-Third streets, loomed up magnificently, as it does still, but it did not draw near it any structures of a like nature, or apparently stimulate building of any kind in the least. It was the pioneer building in the region, but its good work was years in bearing fruit.

CAUSES THAT LED TO THE BUILDING UP OF THE WEST SIDE.

The cause which diverted building from Tenth to Ninth avenue was also the cause of the surprising activity in building on the west side generally—the building of the Ninth Avenue elevated road. With the completion of the road through Ninth Avenue people began to travel over it, often for amusement, from the Battery to 155th street. Many people went over the road that had never been north of Central Park before. They were crowded, many of them, in close, dingy houses on the east side. The universal cry went up: "Why cannot we have better homes? Homes more roomy, better lighted, better ventilated, in this new region?"

There were two reasons why they could not easily. The land on the west side, most of it was owned by speculators, who hold on to their property like grim death, and refused to sell it to anybody. The building of the elevated road forced some of this land out of the hands of these people, and, in a way, made subsequent purchases more easy. But they were still difficult. Besides, the rocky and in some places the swampy condition of the ground made a great many people hesitate about buying real estate there for building purposes. There were engineers who declared that some of the rock was practically irremovable. There were still more engineers who affirmed that if the rock was removed it could only be at enormous cost. The same difficulties were gravely alleged in regard to filling in the low, marshy lots. But all these soon became as naught in the face of the tremendous pressure of the population in the lower part of the city. People crowded each other and declared that they must have elbow room. Homes on the east side became scarce. There was a demand on the part of people, especially young people, for a chance to secure modern homes at moderate prices, which could be purchased on the installment plan. So that those buying might get the benefit of their own savings.

These were the primal causes, undoubtedly, of the building up on the west side. But, by themselves, they would not have been apt to take a clear and effective form. It needed some head, some directing agency. In a little while, after the presence of the need made itself felt in the community, there came to its aid the most practical and efficient helper possible, a vast quantity of unemployed capital in the hands of the great banking and business firms. Such corporations as the Equitable and Mutual Life Insurance Companies eagerly availed themselves of this need and anxiety of the people of the city for homes upon the west side. Private capital, too, was wide-awake. It would be interesting to know just how much money in the early part of 1884 was placed in the hands of real estate agents for the purchase and improvement of land on the west side. The building upon the land since that time, as shown by the illustration, affords, in some degree, at least, a basis for a calculation. When it is remembered that the cost of thousands of new and elegant structures was probably, after all, not greater than the cost of buying and improving the land on which they stood, some idea of the money invested in the west side may be obtained. Real estate brokers were themselves eagerly alive to the situation.

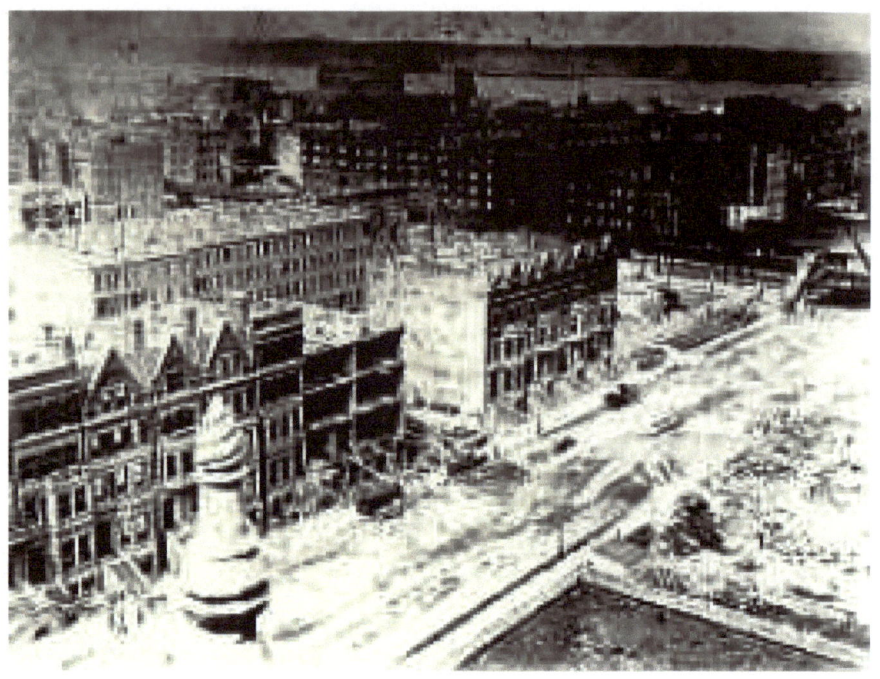

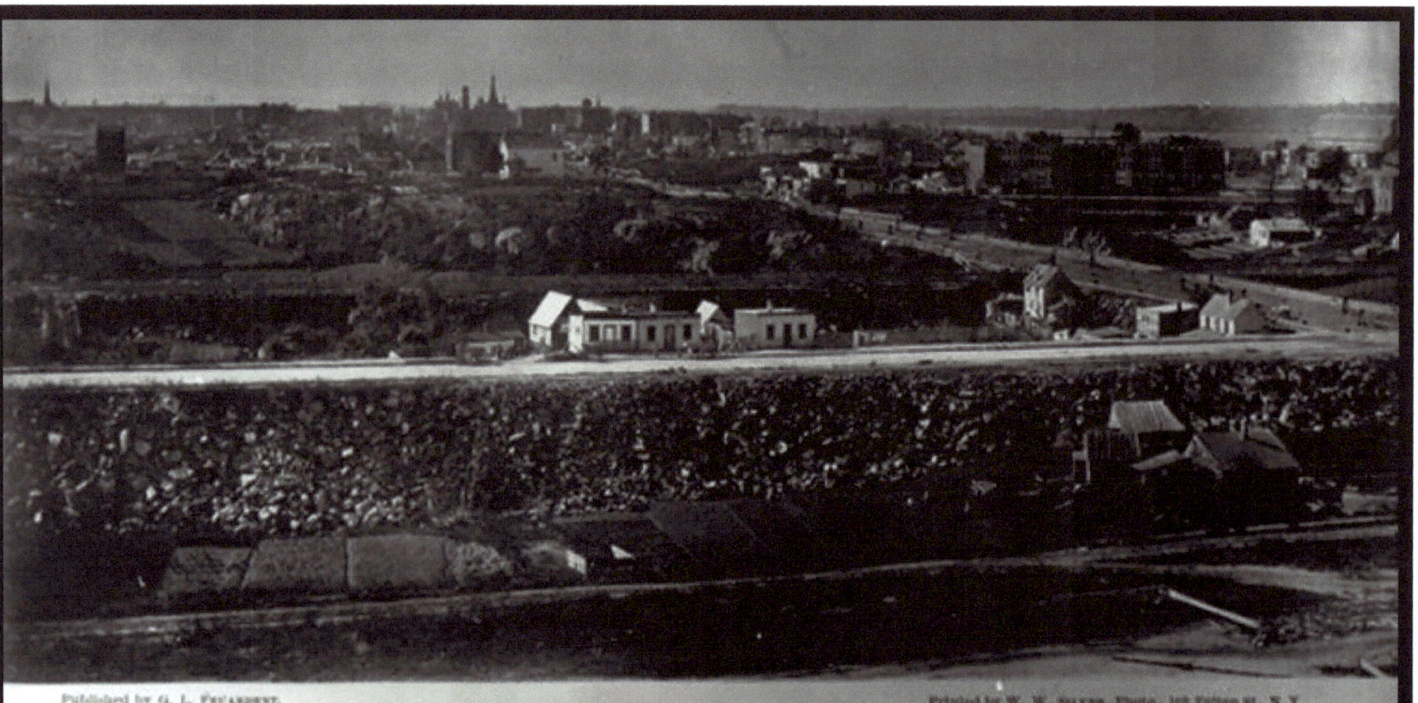

Published by G. L. Feuardent. Printed by W. W. Silver, Photo., 102 Fulton St., N. Y.

PLATE XVII. **PANORAMIC VIEW, WEST OF THE MUSEUM.**

They borrowed largely from the big capitalists, besides using all their own available money. In many instances the banks and others investing money employed agents of their own.

WHO WERE FIRST IN THE FIELD.

Real estate men generally give the credit of the first building on the west side to the Clark estate, or, in reality, the money of the Singer Sewing Machine Company. Mr. Clark was not discouraged by the failure of the Dakota flats to bring about an increase of building near it. In the early part of 1884 he told his friends that the time had come to build, and build he did. He put up in quick succession house after house in Seventy-second and Seventy-third streets. The news-papers praised Mr. Clark for his courage, and printed articles eulogistic of the west side. Then Builders Merritt and Luyster put up beautiful structures in Seventy-Sixth streets and West End Avenue. People were no longer timid. Owners of property stopped looking at each other and saying: "Well, you go on and build, and then I will."

The Equitable Insurance Company invested largely in Harlem and the Mutual Life people in the middle section of the west side. Money went around in the real estate offices at 4 percent, and not a little was lent at 3½ percent, and even at 3¼ percent. The general impression seemed to be among moneyed men that investments on the west side were extremely safe, even if the returns were small at first. Among the real estate men who were quick to see the possibilities and future of the new territory, and who did not have to think twice before investing in property there and advising their customers to invest, were P. H. McManus. Ninth avenue and 135th street: Folsom Brothers, 58 East Thirteenth street: Gnerineau & Drake, 11 Bible House: Wilmot & Jarvis, 1,808 Third avenue; J. Edgar Leaycraft. 1544 Broadway; John R. Foley, 153 Broadway; Just Brothers, 709 Broadway: Anthony Arent, Ninth avenue and Eighty – third street; Joseph Levy & Son, 373 Eight avenue: Morris B. Baer, 72 West Thirty-fourth Street; Brodi & Betty, 1, 216 Third avenue; L. H. da Cunba, Broadway and Forty second street; C. F. Street, 359 West Fifty-ninth street; J. Romaine Brown, 59 West Thirty-third street; Thomas A. Vyse, 66 Liberty street; Potter & Brothers. Ninth avenue and Eighty-second street; Stevens, Ninth avenue and Ninety third street; F. G. Davis, street; Potter & Brothers. Ninth avenue and Eighty-second street; Stevens, Ninth avenue and Ninety third street; F. G. Davis, Ninth avenue, near Ninety-third street, and John H. Blake, 265 Broadway, whose success in developing Brentwood, Long Island, is fresh in the minds of the public. When these men took hold of things people began to come in with a rush, and there was no longer any hesitation.

CHARACTER AND DISTRIBUTION

Building lingered for a while in the neighborhood of Seventy-second Street, where it started, and was for a time confined to residence houses. Then by one of those freaks familiar to people in the real estate business it leaped up to Ninety-third Street, and the building of flats and tenement houses began. Then it came back down town again to Sixty-third and adjacent streets. Since then building has spread in all directions on the west side. Flats, tenement houses and residences have gone up like magic everywhere. An examination of the diagram shows that the Ninth avenue elevated railroad has been the centre of attraction. At first sight it might seem hard to classify the section in regard to the character of the buildings erected, but close inspection shows that the building has progressed steadily and surely within certain very plainly marked lines of development.

Ninth Avenue is the home of tenements, of five and six and even more stories. On the ground floor of these tenements are rooms for stores and other business establishments. People along here say that they want a horse car line badly for local traffic. It is true that the elevated road is there, and that there are surface railroads on all the other avenues. But the Ninth avenue people say that they feel intensely the need of a horse-car line, and that a horse-car line they must have. Of course, tenements have been erected in all parts of the district, but there are more of them around Ninth Avenue than there are anywhere else. The part of each tenement occupied by a family has, as a rule, from four to six rooms, and rents at all the way from $12 to $35 a month. It is hardly fair to say that some of the more costly tenements are not apartment houses. They have carpeted hallways, bathrooms and all the conveniences found in the high-class apartment structure. They are good enough for anybody to live in. A constant improvement is apparent in the new buildings going up. Said Architect and Builder Charles Buek of 1,187 Ninth avenue to a Sun reporter:

"The first buildings erected here in the neighborhood of Seventy-second street are not such as builders would put up now. They are just as strong, of course, but they are not so elegant. Five years ago if we had put up such tenements and apartments as we are now erecting people would have said we were crazy. But now they are satisfied with the buildings erected then. The reason is, of course, that property down here has improved enormously in value since the times of the old buildings, and our new buildings must show a commensurate improvement. The demand is constantly for more elaborate buildings. I think all the people who came here are entirely satisfied. People who came there first did so, in great measure, because they were crowded out of the east side. Now they come here because they like and choose the west side. Rents are going up all the time." The stores beneath the Ninth avenue dwellings rent at $100 to $500 a month.

Eighth Avenue seems as yet to be little built up. Fronting on Central Park, as it does, it will undoubtedly be devoted in future to apartment houses of the first class, such as the Dakota flats, renting for high prices. The retarding of the growth here is ascribed by real estate men to various causes, but the fact seems to be that the land is held for speculative purposes, or rather by people who refuse to sell it, in the hope of a large future rise in value. The holdings of estates here are very large. As yet there has been no severe pressure upon the owners for a sale of their property for building purposes. Most of the people, so far, who have gone up on the west side to live are people of moderate means, who have not demanded the magnificent apartment houses or residences such as Eighth avenue can only be devoted to.

Along Tenth avenue, and to a great extent on corner lots wherever they may be, have been erected what the real estate men known as "good, fair apartment houses." These are, in reality, such elegant structures as the "Ormonde" at Eighty-sixth street and Ninth avenue, built and owned by Prague & Power, the real estate agents who have done so much for Eighty-sixth street and its neighborhood. The tendency seems to be not to go up town in the building of these flats. They stay down below Ninety-sixth Street, though the Shenandoah flats at 135th street and Ninth Avenue, owned by P. H. McManus, the big real estate man of that section, are a notable exception. They rent at $30 to $80 a month. Property in this section is held at first-rate values, and the building is all of a kind that is meant to stay. It is hardly necessary to say that the houses are designed with the utmost care to provide every comfort and luxury. The flats have from six to ten rooms on an average. It is not the fashion longer to give them names.

The cross streets between Fifty-ninth and Ninety-sixth streets are turned over to the residences, through on the corners of these streets have been built some of the more elegant of the flats. The builders of the majority of these houses have put them up with the idea of selling them and they do sell them at anywhere from $35,000 to $60,000. These houses rent at from $1,200 to $2,500 a year a piece. Here, as nowhere else, is the modern character of the building on the west side seen. Every thing about the houses is new and fresh. It is unlike anything in any part of the city. It seems truly the home of the fashionable New Yorker of the future. Nothing can be more picturesque than one of these streets, with its new and varied styles of architecture, its bay and octagonal windows in pretty colored stone, looking out on broad freestone pavements. Often polished ash and oaken handrails lead down the front steps to the sidewalk. The houses, most of them, are built of Jersey and Philadelphia pressed brick. But it is in the facings that the chief beauty and picturesqueness appear. The favorite ones are, besides the popular brown stone, the white limestone and granite, the light brown Belleville stone, the red Lake Superior, and the blue Wyoming. They are carved and fretted into all sorts of pretty designs. The interior decorations of these houses are elaborate. They have permanent fireplace and sideboard fixtures. They are fitted up on the different floors in ash and oak, cherry and walnut, and have hardwood floors. The drawing room floors in many of them are in mosaic. There is no getting around the fact that Seventy-second and Eighty-sixth streets, with Eighty-first and eighty-fourth streets are looked upon just now as the particularly handsome streets in this part of the city.

But it is the West End Avenue and Riverside drives that are going to be the cream and pride of this section. The residences going up there are simply palaces. People who live there are confident that theirs is the future Fifth Avenue of the city. A mere glance at these broad, finely paved avenues and the high ground on which they are located shows the reason for this belief. At present the houses in West End Avenue are mostly between Seventieth and Seventy-sixth streets, but new ones are going up constantly. Property along Riverside drive is still held for speculative purposes, and building there is not progressing rapidly. There are few buildings along the Boulevard, too, from Seventy-sixth Street up.

A PERMANENT AND HEALTHY GROWTH.

Nearly all real estate men agree that this wonderful development of the west side, despite its rapidity, has been steady and natural, and entirely called for by the situation. The growth had not been fictitious. There has been an absurdly small number of business failures in proportion to the almost fabulous amount of money involved. The buildings have been erected in a sound and careful manner. They are preeminently modern, they have been built in accordance with new and severe building and sanitary laws, and every effort has been made to secure safety, roominess, light, and ventilation. Their location is preeminently healthful, standing as it does high above Murray Hill, and almost on a level with the Palisades on the Jersey side of the Hudson. In all this growth there has been no retrograde movement. There have been lulls at times, but nothing of a downfall. The best judgment of experts is that property between Fifty-ninth and Ninety-sixth streets and between Central Park and the North River has increased in value 5o percent, since 1884, and this puts the story in a nutshell. The Ninth avenue elevated railroad is contemplating, and has, in fact, about decided to erect four new stations in this district. This will give another boom to west side property. There are stations now at Fifty-ninth, Seventy-second, Eighty-first. Ninety-third, and 104th streets. The new stations will be at Sixty-sixth, Seventy-sixth, Eighty-sixth, and Ninety-eighth streets.

The Sun,
Saturday, March 23, 1889

THE SUB-SURFACE COURT YARD OF THE "DAKOTA" APARTMENT HOUSE

TO THE EDITORS OF THE AMERICAN ARCHITECT:-

Dear Sir, - I regret being called on so soon again to ask for space in your journal for a correction, but a statement in the article on "Apartment-Houses" in your issue of January, 17, seems to make it necessary.

The author, in referring to the "Dakota," says: "The only criticism to be made upon it, but a serious one, is that the service entrances to the suites are situated upon the same court-yard, so that grocers wagons and ice-cart are almost always to be seen standing about in the space which should lie reserved exclusively for more fashionable equipages, and for the promenades of the tenants of the house."

The fact is, that a grocers' wagon has never been seen within the quiet precincts of this court-yard, and an ice-cart would cause as much consternation to the aristocratic tenants as a street-car trundled into the space. The error, on the part of your author, very probably and naturally arose from not having at hand a basement plan of the building — which I believe has never been published.

Underneath the court, the pavement of which is carried on arches, is a sub-court of precisely the same dimensions, lighted by two large openings, shown on plan. This is reached by a driveway at the rear on Seventy-third Street, of easy incline from the street-level, and a passageway under the building on the westerly side. In this sub-court are received all the commodities of housekeeping and all supplies for the tenants or house proper. The household goods of arriving or departing tenants are here received or discharged, and all garbage or ashes here removed. The service elevators and staircases start from this level, and servants are obliged to enter or leave the house through this court alone.

The arrangement has proved very successful and has attained precisely what your author lamented as lacking, namely, perfect quiet and seclusion for the main court-yard.

Very truly yours,
H. J. HARDENBERGH

American Architect
January 20, 1891

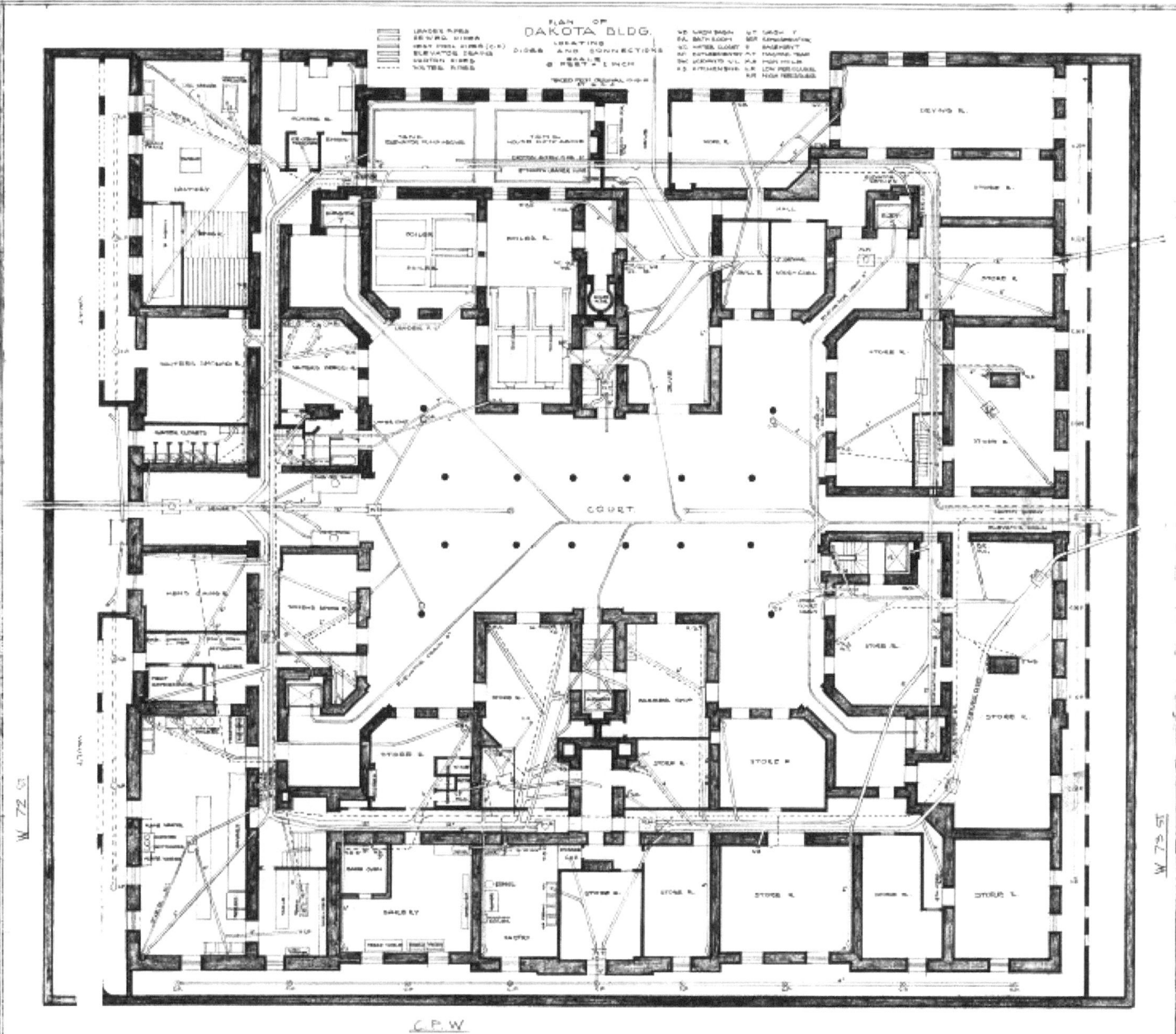

THE "DAKOTA" APARTMENT HOUSE (1884)

THE ARCHITECTURAL RECORD
VOLUME VI
1896/1897

Thirteen years ago the lofty apartment house was an architectural novelty, as the associated apartment house was a novelty in investment. The busiest designers of apartment houses were also the most successful promoters of associations. Upon the whole the architectural results of these operations were much more successful than there was any good reason to expect; much more successful, as everybody knows, than the financial results, which were so discouraging to the investors that for quite a decade nobody has ventured to go about the promotion of a new "associated dwelling."

At any rate, the architectural results were so successful that it is a very considerable distinction to have designed the best apartment house in New York. The Dakota was acclaimed upon its completion of having attained that distinction, which after thirteen years it continues to hold, and which is only emphasized by the erection of newer apartment hotels in its neighborhood, with all the illumination that its design could convey to their designers. The Dakota, of course, was not an associated dwelling, but an individual investment.

The architect had an unusual opportunity in a whole block-front facing Central Park, but the opportunity involved a corresponding responsibility. Central Park is the one municipal possession of which we have a clear right to be proud, and to erect what was in 1883 a towering building of eight stories fronting it, and visible from a great part of it, was for an architect, artistically speaking, to take his life in his hand. Even if he made what in any other place would have been a success, the chances were that the judicious visitor to the Park would prefer nothing in its place, or at least an inconspicuous four-story front which he could ignore. That an eight-story apartment house could become a positive addition to the attractiveness of the Park was an attainment which the architect could scarcely have ventured to promise to himself. Yet in the Dakota this complete success has been attained. The building actually helps the Park.

Its picturesqueness of outline and effect is attained without any sacrifice of unity, or even of formal symmetry, for each front is laterally, as well as vertically, a triple composition, which in both cases is carefully studied in mass and carefully carried out in detail. It is questionable whether the vertical division might not have been still more emphasized to its advantage by constructing the whole of the two-story basement in the olive sandstone which is employed in the wrought work; but the division, emphasized by a broad belt of terra cotta at the impost of the arches and a vigorously moulded string course in stone, is quite unmistakable. Above, the arch-frieze in terra cotta that marks off the roof from the wall does not lack emphasis.

The lateral division, into a central and two terminal pavilions, is almost equally effective whether the central feature is crowned with a steep hood, relieved with a crow-stepped dome and rows of spire lights, on the avenue front, or carried up into a picturesque gable on the street front. Though the projection of the pavilions is slight, they are effectually detached by the plainer treatment of the strips of curtain wall, by the separate and subordinate roofing of these, and by the omission from them of the corbeled cornice with its balcony. All the features are successfully studied, noticeably the seven-story oriels of the end pavilions on the street front. The detail is avowedly eclectic, and the general reminder the building gives of the French transitional is due much more to the picturesque composition than to the detail. One might wish for a more vigorous modeling of this detail, especially for a more forcible expression of depth in the modeling in the openings. A certain flatness prevents the design from making its full effect. But this is the sole drawback, and it does not prevent the Dakota from being by far the most considerable, architecturally, of all the apartment houses.

The agreeableness of its composition and its detail is much enhanced by the agreeableness of its combination of color, the olive sandstone being employed in conjunction with a salmon-colored brick, and the darker tint being used with unfailing structural propriety to accentuate the design.

Architectural Record
1896/1897

N.Y.'s First Big Apartment House – Built in 1881

THE EVENING WORLD
DAILY MAGAZINE
MAY 13, 1919

THE DAKOTA
CORNER CENTRAL PARK WEST AND SEVENTY–SECOND STREET AS IT APPEARED WHEN COMPLETED THIRTY – EIGHT YEARS AGO AND VIEW OF BLOCK BELOW SHOWING CHARACTER OF SURROUNDINGS IN THOSE DAYS.

RISING ten stories high amid the lowly homes of Shantytown, the Dakota, New York City's first apartment house of any pretentiousness, was built in 1881, in Central Park West at 72d Street. Despite its thirty-eight years of age, it is still occupied by some of the wealthiest and most exclusive families of the city.

When the artist for The Evening World drew and contributed the drawing to Leslie's back in 1889 the little truck gardeners were still obtaining their living from their cabbage patches, while goats and ducks and chickens and pigs, too, roamed at will as part of the domestic blessings of the shantytown residents. The Dakota was bounded on the north and south by these bumble cottagers.

The building was designed by Henry Janeway Hardenbergh, the architect who built the Hotel Plaza here and the William Hotel in Washington. It is owned by the Clark estate, whose fortune was made in sewing machines. The estate owns apartment properties, it is said, which are valued at $12,000,000.

Rentals in the Dakota have kept pace with the times, and the high character of its tenants has been maintained throughout all the years of its existence. It is modernized as programs in modern dwellings is made, and according to real estate agents the rentals are as high as those of the most recently built apartment houses.

The Dakota is noted among real estate men for its remarkably high ceilings. They are 13 feet high, while the average apartment house room is only 10 ½ feet from floor to ceiling. This added height makes the apartment as tall as the average twelve story building in the city.

The building is constructed of brown brick trimmed with chocolate colored stone. The interior decorations are said to be very rich, black walnut being used in the woodwork. There is a restaurant which is very exclusive. It is patronized only by the tenants of the building and few outside of the Dakota know that a cafe exists there.

There are a number of three and four room apartments and the roof is planted with grass and shrubbery. It is in fact a tiny park.

Since the erection of the Dakota many more buildings have risen along Central Park West, but the pioneer of them all stands sturdily maintaining its position of leader. Real estate men estimate that the rentals in the Dakota run about $4,500 a year, which they say is about equal to that charged in the more recently constructed buildings.

There was only one other apartment at the time the Dakota was built. It was the Van Corlear in Seventh Avenue, between 55th and 56th Streets. It was smaller and was also designed by Hardenbergh, the architect of the Dakota.

Some of the newer apartments have more pretentious entrances, and the apartments are provided with more rooms and baths for servants than when the Dakota was built, but in all else the Dakota is their peer.

Biography of Edward Clark

EDWARD CLARK

THE REAL ESTATE RECORD & GUIDE

Mr. Clark was born at Athens, Greene Co., N.Y., Dec. 19, 1811. His father, Nathan Clark, a successful manufacturer, still resides there, at the advanced age of ninety-one years. His mother was the daughter of John Nichols, of Waterbury, Conn., of the same family as Richard Nichols, cammande of the expeditionary force, by which the city of New York was taken from the Dutch. Passing over his early years and academicals training, we find he graduated from William's College in 1830, and the same year entered the law office of Ambrose L. Jordan, Esq., at Hudson, N. Y., a city then distinguished as a school for intended lawyers.

In 1833, he began the practice of law in Poughkeepsic, and, in 1837, formed a law partnership with Mr. Jordan, and commenced a successful practice in this city.

In the year 1848, Isaac M. Singer, one of their clients, an erratic genius, having followed various occupations without much success, and invented valuable mechanical devices which brought no profit, was a client of Messrs. Jordan & Clark, and, shortly after this time, made his great invention of the Sewing Machine. Under the management of the inventor, the title to the invention became involved and was likely to be lost.

In an emergency, Singer applied to his legal adviser, Clark, to advance the means to prosecute the business successfully, and thereupon was formed the co-partnership of I. M. Singer and Co, with evident success from 1851 to 1868.
It was during these years of costly and vexatious law suits, and faced by hostile injunctions, that, under the management and direction of Mr. Clark, the contest was perseveringly maintained, the business continued to prosper, and defensive litigation terminated. It is known that the early management of the business, and the direction given to it in the beginning by Mr. Clark, have contributed to its present permanent success and celebrity.

In 1863, wishing to be relieved from active duty, and desiring to secure its contained good management, he conceived the scheme of organizing, "The Singer Manufacturing Company," and, upon its formation that year, though a director, retired from active management, and, during several years, spent considerable time abroad.

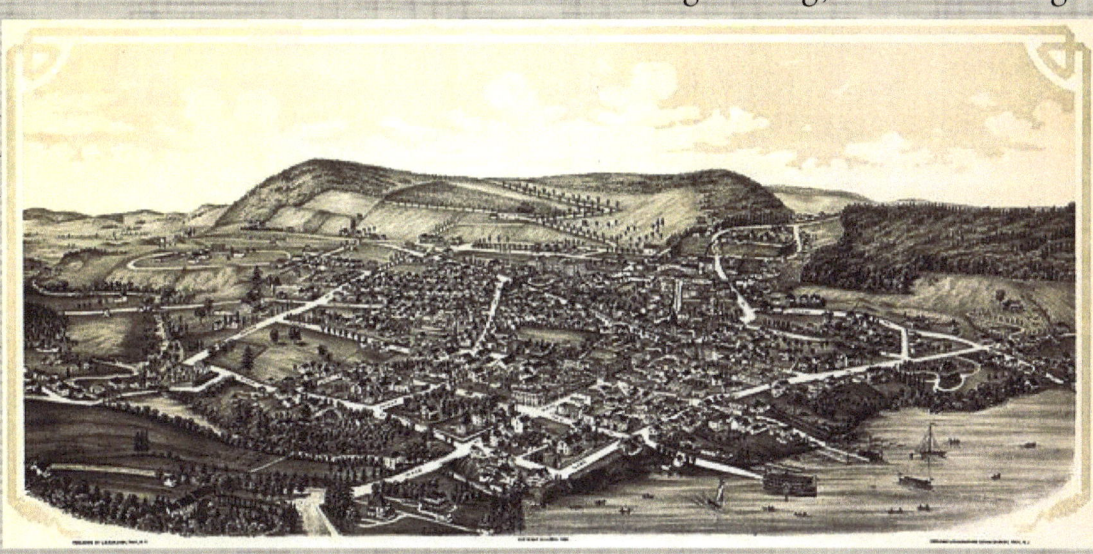

In his travels over Europe, he examined what over was worthy of notice in nature and art, and had full and lengthened experience of the various methods of living in hotels and rented in the principal cities of those countries.

In the autumn of 1854, he fixed his residence in the village of Cooperstown, Otsego County, N. Y., and has continued to reside there ever since.

He purchased, at that time, the dwelling known as "Apple Hill," formerly owned by Geo A. Starkweather, and by Richard Cooper, and occupied at various times by Hon. John A. Dix, Hon. Samuel Nelson, Judge I. C. Turner and others. This building was torn down, and a new stone one occupies its place. It and the grounds now called "Fernleigh." in the guidebooks this house is extravagantly praised, and few strangers visit Coppers town without seeking to see it.

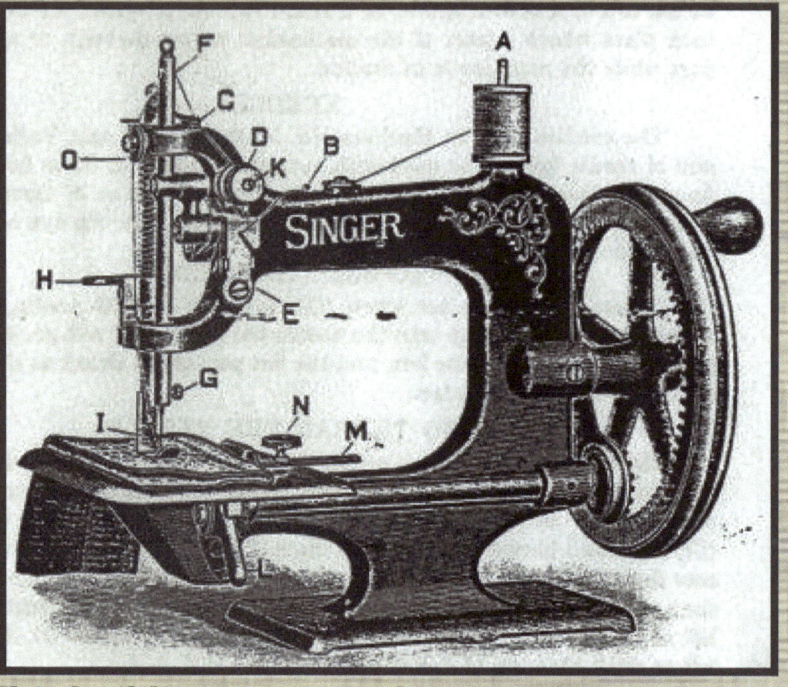

We have passed over his professional carrier in the city, in great part occupied by the care necessary over the interests of the firm above mentioned. Constantly on the alert for new moves, and called on incessantly for professional advice, he was quick to perceive and prompt in action. The partner of the late Ambrose L. Jordan, he was obliged to share and assist in the labors of that distinguished gentleman and lawyer. From 1838 to 1860 the firm of Jordan & Clark was retained and prominently engaged in a large proportion of the severely instigated cases which occupied the Courts of New York, and were opposed by some of the form most advocates of the New York Bar.

Having done, and still continuing to do his part for the improvement of Cooperstown, his home and residence, Mr. Clarke has now turned his attention to this city, the scene of his early labors and successes.

Isaac Merritt Singer

THE NEW YORK TIMES
PUBLISHED: JULY 25, 1875

ISAAC MERRITT SINGER died on Thursday last at Torquay, a well-known watering place in England. Mr. Singer was in part the inventor, and was also the manufacturer, of the sewing- machine which bears his name. He was born in Owego, N. Y., Oct. 27, 1811, and was by trade a machinist. Early in his career as a workman he made himself familiar with all that had been made known concerning the manufacture of sewing- machines. He gave to their construction his undivided attention for several years in Boston, where he encountered great difficulties in his progress in the work of producing a machine which he could call his own. At length he moved to New-York, perfected his machine, and opened a manufactory in what was then known as the Harlem Railroad Depot building, in Centre street, between Franklin and Worth. During his earlier efforts, and until about 1850, his means were small— so slender, indeed, that he had become almost hopeless of reaching success. About that time, however, he succeeded in securing both the sympathy and services of a wealthy lawyer named Edward Clark, who secured his patents for him and advanced the money he needed to enable him to go on with his work. His first machine was what became known as a single thread chain-

stitch machine. In opposition to his was the lock-stitch machine of Elias Howe who had control of the Walter Hunt patent for manufacturing what was known as the double lock- stitch shuttle machine. With the Howe Company he had serious difficulty; he was charged with having infringed upon their patents, and long and costly suits followed, which were prominent features in the newspapers of that time. The Hunt patent proved too strong for him to break. After having gone through the courts without receiving a satisfactory decision, Mr. Singer finally succeeded in effecting a compromise, and was then allowed to proceed. His business difficulties were not yet ended, however, for he was soon in trouble with his moneyed friend and lawyer, Mr. Clark, a trouble which was not settled until both had agreed, while retaining equal interest in the patents, to resign all control of the manufacturing and other business departments into the hands of a company, of which Mr. Iuslee A. Hopper was President. In the hands of the company the business proved a great success, and the profits which were awarded to Singer made him, years ago, a wealthy man. But again, as poverty and business difficulties disappeared, family troubles came upon him. He went abroad, going to reside in Paris, but the Communists made it unpleasant for him, and he went to England. At Torquay he erected a very costly and curiously constructed building for a residence, and in it he lived and died.

Three of his sons are in business in this City, and there are other children elsewhere.

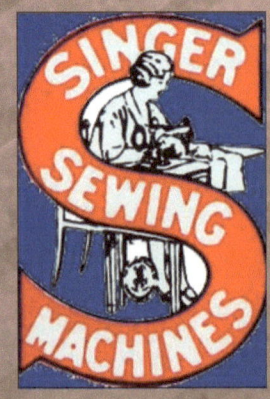

Henry Janeway Hardenbergh

ARCHITECTURAL RECORD
JULY, 1896 - JUNE, 1897

HENRY JANEWAY HARDENBERGH was born at New Brunswick, N. J., Feb. 6, 1847, although his family moved, when he was two years old, and he has since resided in Jersey City and New York City. He comes of the Dutch stock which has been so potent in the development of New Jersey. His first American ancestor emigrated from Amsterdam about 1644. His great great grandfather, Jacob Rutsen Hardenbergh, was one of the founders of Queen's, now Rutgers, College and became its first President in 1785.

In 1865 Mr. Hardenbergh entered the office of Detlef Lienau, a German by birth and temperament, and both German and French by professional training. He was a pupil of Henri Labrouste and had imbibed in that atelier a partial belief in the neo-grec of which his "patron" was the apostle. Mr. Lienau's professional work in New York was not so extensive as it deserved to be. A glass warehouse of his design in Howard street was for many years after its erection one of the most interesting and respectable of our commercial buildings, with touches of the neo-grec in detail that did it neither much good nor much harm, but with the evidence of artistic sense and training in its proportion and its fenestration, and with a straightforward and structural treatment throughout, that were very rare then and are not very common now. This work was seriously marred by the addition of a story or two, I know not whether or not by the original architect, but at any rate a necessary disturbance of a design already complete. By the same author was evidently also an office building in Cedar street, much later in date, though still before the elevator had begun to work its influence on the design of commercial buildings, and by no

Geology Hall (1872)

"This brownstone structure was designed by Henry Janeway Harctenbergb, the great-great-grandson of Rutgers' first president. The building served as home to the departments of physics, military science and geology. The Rutgers Geological Museum, housed on the second floor, has included important collections of minerals, fossils, Native American artifacts, modem shells, and a 10,000-year-old mastodon acquired by Professor George H. Cook in 1870." (Exterior plaque)

Rutgers College Kirkpatrick Chapel (1873)

means so successful in composition, though it had the same attractiveness of a rational following out of the ground-plan in the elevation, and of a straightforward and structural treatment of detail. I recall nothing else of Mr. Lienau's in New York, though on the Jersey side of the North River he erected some warehouses that were very conspicuous objects in the skyline of that low shore before it was as crowded as it has since become.

Mr. Lienau's neo-grec had no great influence on his pupil, as it has long ceased to have any influence on any designers, although the first of Mr. Hardenbergh's apartment houses, the Van Corlear on Seventh avenue, shows in some of its details the efforts of his special studies. Much more than in detail it reveals them in what I am compelled, for want of a better word, to call the spottiness of effect which seems to belong to all the neo-grec work done on this side of the water, at least. Nothing could be more remote from the quietness which the architect has cultivated and attained in his riper work than this jerky and detonating style. Mr. Lienau's own work in it was by no means so explosive as the early works in it of Mr. Hunt, who was the apostle of it in New York. But Mr. Lienau's work shows qualities that were quite independent of this special style, and that were calculated to be of great advantage to an apt pupil. Chief among them was what I have called the straightforward and structural treatment of his designs, the habit of considering the artistic problem as inextricably connected with the mechanical problem, of regarding his paper design as the drawing of a building rather than the execution of it as the building of a drawing. When Mr. Hardenbergh was graduated from Mr. Lienau's office, "Victorian Gothic" was in full possession of the aspiring and active minded of the younger American architects. Of this, his first work, the building for the grammar school of Rutgers College (1870) was more or less an example.

Three years later, however, a more important and more significant work, the combined chapel and library of the college, is Gothic, indeed, but no more of the "Victorian" variety than it is neo-grec. It is even quite as much German as English Gothic, deriving its German character chiefly from the composition and detail of one of its most attractive features, the triple porch, with its tall pointed openings without exterior mouldings, its buttresses produced through the parapet and crowned with finials,and the gable-mouldings similarly produced and crowned. It is still a creditable piece of work, which is so straightforwardly designed that it cannot conceivably become ridiculous with any change in its surroundings and that it harmonizes with the surroundings for which it was designed in spite of the want of technical congruity of its style.

Adelaide Apartment House (1887)

As the work of a young architect, almost a beginner in 1873, it is remarkable, considering what the ambitious and modish young architects of that time were doing, for its renunciation of the kind of effect and the means of effectiveness which most of them sought. It would not be just to call its sober monochrome dull, for there is no lack of animation in the composition. But it shows that the designer was less afraid of dulness than of restlessness, and it shows that he was more impressed than his

Western Union Telegraph Company's Building (1883)

contemporaries were apt to be with "the value of peace and quietness." He has continued ever since to exhibit his appreciation of those excellent qualities.

It was ten years later, after a variety of professional employments that were mainly useful to the architect, artistically speaking, as studies, that Mr. Hardenbergh began to produce a series of works which showed unmistakably that he had "found his handwriting;" that he had attained the power of putting an individual stamp upon his handiwork. This proclamation was made most powerfully, though not quite first, in the Dakota, which is of special significance in that we may suppose that the success of it determined its author's special "line" as a builder of hotels, in which his most conspicuous work has since been done.

Architectural Record
July, 1896 - June, 1897

Waldorf Astoria (1893)

Plaza Hotel (1907)
5th Avenue, New York City.

The John Wolfe Building (1895)
Maiden lane and William St., New York City.

The Astor Building (1885)
Wall St., New York City.

Dwellings (1883)
West 73rd St., New York City.

www.ingramcontent.com/pod-product-compliance
Lightning Source LLC
Chambersburg PA
CBHW042006150426
43194CB00003B/139